THE
SHAPING
OF
SHETLAND

THE
SHAPING
OF
SHETLAND

Edited by Val Turner

Published by
The Shetland Times Ltd.,
Lerwick.
1998

First published by The Shetland Times Ltd., 1998

ISBN 1 898852 32 4

British Library Cataloguing-in-Publication Data
A catalogue record for this book is
available from the British Library.

Printed and published by
The Shetland Times Ltd,
Prince Alfred Street,
Lerwick,
Shetland. ZE1 0EP.

CONTENTS

ILLUSTRATIONS

CONTRIBUTORS

Simon Butler   is an Honorary Research Fellow in the School of Geography, University of Birmingham and managing director of "Hidden History Tours".

John Hunter   is the Professor of the Department of Ancient History and Archaeology at the University of Birmingham.

Olwyn Owen   is an Inspector of Ancient Monuments with Historic Scotland.

Mike Canter   is an independent archaeologist, living in Bigton, Shetland.

Steve Dockrill   lectures in the School of Archaeological Sciences, University of Bradford.

Julie Bond   is the post-excavation co-ordinator for the Old Scatness Broch project, based at the University of Bradford.

Terry O'Connor   lectures in environmental archaeology in the School of Archaeological Sciences, University of Bradford.

Robert Leask   is a local historian and a member of Nesting Local History Group.

Andy Bradley   is treasurer of Nesting Local History Group and is currently exploring and restoring the old croft buildings of Gletness.

Jennie Bradley   is chairperson of Nesting Local History Group and is currently exploring and restoring the old croft buildings of Gletness.

William Thomson   is a local historian and retired headmaster of Kirkwall Grammar School.

Stephen Carter   is a director of Headland Archaeology Ltd., Edinburgh.

Donald Davidson   lectures in the Department of Environmental Science, University of Stirling.

Val Turner   is the Shetland Archaeologist and Honorary Research Fellow in the School of Archaeological Sciences, University of Bradford.

INTRODUCTION

Val Turner

The archaeology of Shetland is spectacular: where else can a visitor see 4,000 years of the past on one site as can be seen at Jarlshof, or climb up 13m of broch as at Mousa? The most remarkable feature of Shetland archaeology does not however, lie in these individual monuments alone, but in the fact that these monuments are situated within landscapes which have largely been untouched in recent times. Alasdair Whittle was one of the first academics to realise this when he carried out excavation and survey work at the Scord of Brouster near the Bridge of Walls in the late 1970s (published 1986). Indeed, the West Side of Shetland contains mile after mile of prehistoric landscapes which still await systematic study.

The reason for the exceptional state of preservation of the archaeology of Shetland is that so much of the land is what can be described as "marginal". In other words, it will support people if the climate is good and no disasters strike, but the risks involved are high. As the soil became exhausted and the climate deteriorated, peat began to encroach from the hill tops, and much of the land became unrewarding to use for agriculture. Throughout Shetland generally there was a move towards sheep farming, and so even on the richer land, the relics of earlier times have not been ploughed out. Remains which, were they in the south of England, would exist today only as cropmarks visible from the air for a day or two every few years, in Shetland can be stumbled across in the hills, perfectly visible to the casual observer.

It is now ten years since I was appointed to the newly created post of Shetland Archaeologist, within Shetland Amenity Trust. Those ten years have also seen the appreciation of the outstanding quality of Shetland's archaeology grow and grow, both in Shetland and further afield. Our relatively intact landscapes have been studied by an increasing number of people. One, very deliberate, attempt to raise people's awareness, was the "Shetland Settlement" conference, organised by Shetland Archivist, Brian Smith, and myself, in 1988. An earlier version of three of the papers in this volume were written for that conference (Owen, Hunter, Thomson). The creation of the Shetland Sites and Monuments Record has formed the basis for studying the landscape over the last ten years. It has enabled people to begin to understand how Shetland developed as a whole, rather then just concentrating on individual sites. The remains in Shetland are, however, so rich that the Sites and Monuments Record is insufficient on its own. Landscape surveys have been, and still are, required in order to enhance our understanding of how Shetland was shaped.

Shetland has been lucky enough, or attractive enough, to entice some of the very best landscape archaeologists and historians to her shores during the last 10 years. Olwyn Owen's survey of Kebister and Simon Butler's environmental work arising from it, together with John Hunter's survey of Fair Isle, were early leaders in the field. More recently, Steve Dockrill et al's work in South Nesting and

1

Stephen Carter's work in Papa Stour, have been at the cutting edge of archaeological science. Shetland Amenity Trust and Bradford University are now continuing to develop these techniques, in a multifaceted excavation and survey in the South Mainland, centred on Old Scatness Broch and the area around Jarlshof. Meanwhile, William Thomson has been one of the first people to study the historic landscape; more recently Robert Leask, Andy Bradley and Jennie Bradley have examined a crofting landscape. Their paper shows just how important local knowledge is, and just how much oral history and the work of local history groups have to contribute to what we know about the recent past. Following a different line of study, local archaeologist, Mike Canter, has applied computer techniques — Geographic Information Systems — in order to develop work on the Bronze Age landscape further. My hope is that this collection of papers will inspire more people: local individuals and groups, Shetland residents, professionals, students and visitors, to discover the richness of Shetland's past for themselves.

In conclusion, I would like to thank Catrina MacInnes for slaving over a hot keyboard to put these papers together, also my colleagues, and the Shetland residents, too numerous to mention, who have helped, encouraged and contributed so much to my work over the past ten years. Unfortunately four of these people have died in the past two years: Dr T. M. Y. Manson, Rhoda Bulter, Geordie Gear and, most recently, Bobby Tulloch. Their memory will, however, continue to be an encouragement over the coming ten years.

A Note on Dating

Most of the dates referred to in this volume are approximate, based on site typology (shape, etc.) rathern than radiocarbon dating. Where radiocarbon dates are used they appear as lower—case "b.c." or "a.d." dates in the uncalibrated form (±). This is because radiocarbon dates are known to be too young as given by laboratories and there is not yet a definitive system for correcting them.

Simon Butler's paper uses "BP" dates. These dates are calculated as being "Before Present", i.e. how many years ago events took place. "Present" for these purposes is taken as being 1950, which was when nuclear testing began to significantly alter the amount of background radiocarbon in the atmosphere.

An Approximate Scheme of Dating for Prehistoric Shetland

c.7000 BC	Pollen evidence suggests brief presence of Mesolithic (Middle Stone Age hunter-gatherers) in Shetland
3500 b.c.	Earliest dated Neolithic structure in Shetland (a dyke at Shurton Brae) so far
1800 BC	Bronze Age
800 BC	Early Iron Age
400BC-400 AD	Middle Iron Age (Broch Period)
400-900 AD	Late Iron Age (Wheelhouse + Pictish Period)
900 AD	Viking Period

CLIMATE, ECOLOGY AND LAND-USE SINCE THE LAST ICE AGE

Simon Butler

Introduction

At the height of the last Ice Age, some 18,000 years ago, Shetland was frozen beneath a thick capping of ice. Global climatic warming led to the complete melting of this ice by c.10,000 years ago, and allowed recolonisation of the islands by plants, animals and human groups. The aim of this paper is to describe the environmental changes and ecological developments which have taken place in Shetland during the last c.10,000 years, and to highlight how the landscape has been shaped and changed during this time by a combination of natural and cultural influences. This 'postglacial' period is referred to as the 'Holocene' period.

Shetland Palynology

A range of techniques are available for investigating environmental changes during the Holocene period, and one of the most powerful techniques for Shetland has been that of fossil pollen analysis, often referred to as 'palynology'. The hard outer shell of pollen grains is far more resistant to decay over time than other plant parts, and it may survive in ancient sediments for many thousands of years. Plant types (taxa) produce distinctive looking pollen grains, and it is possible to identify the plant species, genus or family from which the pollen was derived. By extracting fossil pollen from ancient sediments, and by quantifying the relative amounts of different types in sediments of different ages, it is possible to gain an understanding of vegetation and land-use changes through time, and to infer the interrelations between plants and other elements of landscape, such as climate, soils and human activity.

The most important types of ancient sediment for palynology are lake and peat deposits, and the widespread occurrence of these within Shetland provides remarkable potential for developing an extensive network of well-stratified pollen profiles. Fig 1. shows the distribution of sites in Shetland from which Holocene pollen profiles have so far been produced. Interpretation of each profile has aimed to produce a time-sequence of vegetational and related ecological changes at the site. The most common dating method for these changes has been radiocarbon dating of the organic sediment which they lie in. Most of the pollen at each site will have come from within less than a few kilometres radius of the site, but correlation and comparison of dated pollen-profiles from different sites enables us to build-up a regional-scale view of landscape changes across the Islands. Where sites are

3

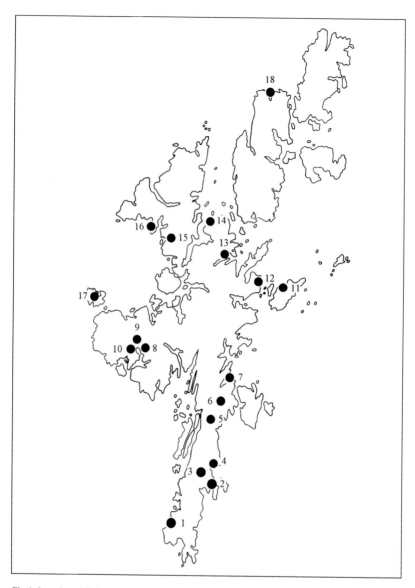

Fig 1. Location of Holocene Pollen Sites in Shetland. 1. Spiggie (Birnie, 1981); 2. Leebotten (Birnie, 1981); 3. Ward of Veester (Birnie, 1984); 4. Aith Voe (Birnie, 1981); 5. Lang Lochs (Hulme and Durno, 1980); 6. Shurton Hill (Whittington, 1980); 7. Kebister (Butler, 1992); 8. Murraster (Johansen, 1975); 9. Scord of Brouster (Keith-Lucas, 1986); 10. Loch of Brunatwatt (Edwards and Moss, 1993); 11. Symbister Bay (Hoppe, 1965); 12. Dallican Water (Bennett *et. al.*, 1992); 13. The Houb (Birnie, 1981); 14. Garths Voe (Birnie, 1981, 1993); 15. Gunnister (Bennett *et. al.*, 1993); 16. Hillswick (Birnie, 1981); 17. Papa Stour (Whittington and Edwards, 1993); 18. Breckin, Yell (Birnie, 1984).

4

located close to archaeological remains they can provide detailed information about land-use changes and human-environment relations.

The Earlier Holocene (c.10,000-5,000 BP)

The climate improved rapidly over north-west Europe during the tenth millennium BP. By 9,000 BP the temperature was probably similar to that of today, and it would have risen another 1-3° by 8,000 BP (Birks, 1986; Lamb, 1988). During these first two millennia of the Holocene period, mainland Britain and continental Europe generally saw the immigration, expansion and eventual dominance of temperate deciduous trees, and the development of fertile brown-earth soils. With the development of a thickening soil, increased vegetational cover and more constant climatic conditions, Holocene environments gradually became more 'stable'.

The Shetland Islands lay at the exposed, Atlantic, north-western margin of the extensive European mixed-deciduous forests, and fossil pollen evidence from Shetland indicates that Holocene woodland development here was less well pronounced than in other parts of Europe. Total tree and shrub pollen values rarely exceed c. 70% of the total pollen present in Holocene pollen profiles from Shetland, which tends to suggest a fairly open, light covering of woodland. The range of native arboreal taxa also appears quite restricted, with birch (*Betula*), hazel (*Corylus avellana*), willow (*Salix*), rowan (*Sorbus aucuparia*) and juniper (*Juniperus communis*) as the main types. The status of other tree/shrub taxa, notably alder (*Alnus glutinosa*), oak (*Quercus*), pine (*Pinus*), elm (*Ulmus*), ash (*Fraxinus*) and aspen (*Populus tremula*) is less certain due to their low fossil pollen frequencies and a lack of fossil wood remains, but the local presence of at least some of these taxa (particularly alder and oak) cannot be ruled-out, and they may have created a more diverse woodland flora than palynologists have traditionally envisaged for Shetland (Bennett et. al., 1992).

Some local variation in Holocene woodland communities is detectable in the pollen assemblages from different sites in Shetland, and further variations seem likely to appear as more sites are analysed. Birch (*Betula*) is the most consistently well represented tree taxon, and was probably Shetland's most common native tree on account of its wide ecological tolerance. It is clear from buried soil pollen assemblages that hazel (*Corylus avellana*) was dominant in places, probably on less acidic soils which subsequently proved valuable for agricultural settlement. Phases of willow (*Salix*) fen development are evidenced on wetter soils, and at some sites juniper (*Juniperus communis*) became periodically important. The native ground flora of the woodlands generally comprised of ferns and tall herbs such as grasses (Poaceae), umbellifers (Umbelliferae), meadowsweet (*Filipendula ulmaria*), dandelions (Compositae Liguliflorae), willowherbs (*Epilobiun*), and nettles (*Urtica*). Again, local variations in the ground flora are evidenced in the pollen records.

The upper limit of Shetland's woodland appears to have lain at approximately 200m OD, suggesting that most of the land area of the islands would have been able to support tree growth (Spence, 1979). Above the tree-line it seems likely that a range of heathland, montane grassland and fell-field plant communities would have been found. Less fertile soils would also have occurred naturally in poorly-drained areas of the lowlands, where fen and bog plant communities may have grown on waterlogged gley and peaty soils, and also in freely-draining areas with acidic rocks where a lack of base nutrients may have favoured species-poor heathland on leached podsols.

Archaeological evidence pre-dating the start of the Neolithic period (c. 5000 BP) has so far been conspicuously absent from the Shetland Islands, and palynological evidence for Pre-Neolithic human interference with the vegetation cover has been similarly elusive. Bennett et al. (1992) have recently suggested that changes in the ground and shrub flora around 7500 BP, recorded as a decline in ferns, meadowsweet (*Filipendula*) and Juniper (*Juniperus*) and Crowberry (*Empetrum*) shrubs in their Dallican Water profile, may have been caused by the first appearance in Shetland of grazing mammals such as red deer. The authors drew attention to the fact that hunting of red deer by Mesolithic cultures is well attested throughout Britain, and that increases in microscopic charcoal representation at Dallican Water might reflect the local use of fire by Mesolithic people.

The Later Holocene (c. 5000 BP to present)

The most notable event in Shetland's environmental history during the later Holocene is the loss of the native woodland and tall-herb communities and their associated brown-earth soils, and their replacement by widespread heathland communities on acid podsols and blanket peats. There are signs at most sites for increasing soil acidification from about the seventh millennium BP, and for peat inception at various times during the Holocene, but the most dramatic and permanent vegetation changes are recorded during the fifth, fourth and third millennia BP. These take the form of declines in tree and shrub pollen frequencies and increases in herbaceous and heathland pollen frequencies. By the third millennium BP the environment of Shetland seems to have become significantly impoverished, with extensive areas of podsolised peaty soils, blanket peats, and species-poor heathland or acid grassland. Woodlands and tall-herb meadows were becoming scarce, and Shetland's natural environment was approaching the type of landscape seen today.

Shetland's naturally moist climate produces a natural tendency over time towards soil leaching, acidification and podsolisation, and it is clear that peat formation and retrogression from woodland to acid heathland can follow on naturally from podsolisation (Moore, 1988). To some extent therefore, Shetland was destined to experience these ecological changes without any need for external causes such as climatic deterioration or human impact. There is however pollen evidence to show that prehistoric human activity did have considerable impact on the environment, and it is also clear that some climatic deterioration has taken place.

Human Impact

The introduction of Neolithic farming during the fifth millennium BP seems to have had a significant impact on the landscape. Palynological evidence for Neolithic clearance of the native woodland and tall-herb and fern communities, and their replacement with grassy pasture, arable plots and heathland, has been dated at the Scord of Brouster to c. 4680 BP (Keith-Lucas, 1986). Bone preservation was poor at the site, but there was evidence for the presence of cattle, sheep and red deer. A mixed-farming Neolithic settlement practising a form of infield-outfield agriculture has been suggested for the site. Nearby at Murraster the woodland decline is dated to c. 4650 BP, and the associated increase in plantain (*Plantago lanceolata*) here again suggests that early agricultural activity was the cause (Johansen, 1975, 1978, 1985). At Kebister the decline in woodland and tall herbs and ferns took place before c. 4540 BP, and is associated with pollen and charcoal evidence for human activity (Butler, 1992). At Dallican Water (Bennett et al., 1992) woodland clearance took place at c. 4000 BP, whilst at Gunnister (Bennett et al., 1993) the vegetation seems to have remained largely unaffected by human activity until the Later Bronze Age, c. 3000 BP.

Survey evidence from the West Side demonstrates that there was a well-filled prehistoric landscape of dispersed farming settlements [Whittle et al. (1986), Fojut (1986)]. Fojut ascribes many of the large dykes, some of which run across country for many miles, to the Neolithic or Bronze Age period and points to their implications in terms of a well organised farming society and landscape. More radiocarbon dates are required from these dyke systems, but Whittington (1980) obtained a radiocarbon date of c. 4740 BP from the buried soil beneath a stone-built dyke on Shurton Hill, thereby indicating that the dyke itself is probably of Neolithic or Bronze Age construction.

Prehistoric settlement at the Scord of Brouster was characterised by approx. 500 years of Early Neolithic mixed-farming followed by a short phase of reduced activity, during which there is evidence for some reversion of farmland to scrub. Renewed clearance during the Later Neolithic at c. 4180 BP appears to have heralded a phase lasting well into the Bronze Age during which there was an expansion of heathland around the site and the land-use emphasis shifted more towards pastoral use of the heath rather than arable farming, although arable farming does continue. Whittle et al. (1986) have suggested that this change in land-use emphasis might reflect a response to a changing environment, particularly declining soil productivity.

At Kebister there was also an expansion of heathland pasture during the Later Neolithic period. High quantities of charcoal and good pollen representation of herbs such as tormentil (*Potentilla*) and ribwort plantain (*Plantago lanceolata*) here suggest a species-rich grazed and burnt heath in which the growth of heather was deliberately kept in check in order to provide pasture suitable for all year round grazing. Pollen and charcoal analyses from Shurton Hill and from the Ward of Veester also suggest areas of Neolithic or Bronze Age heathland pasture maintained by muir-burning. Shetland heaths are still grazed and burnt today, and Kaland (1986) has suggested that this type of heath farming is a traditional form of land management widespread in Atlantic heath areas since Neolithic times. He suggests that some areas of heathland may have been deliberately created or extended as part of early mixed farming systems, in which the heathy outfield pastures were complemented by cultivation of infield areas closer to the farm buildings.

Most pollen profiles from Shetland register increasing amounts of heather (*Calluna vulgaris*) pollen during Bronze Age times, often replacing the more species-rich Neolithic heathland. Whilst controlled grazing and burning improve soil fertility and species-diversity in the short-term, the long-term effects can be detrimental if practised without care, leading to the dominance of heather, soil acidification, waterlogging and peat growth (Moore, 1988). As Whittington (1980) points out, there is a possibility that the over-grazing and over-burning of Shetland's heathlands during prehistory could have encouraged the spread of heather dominated peatlands at a time when climatic and soil formation processes were already causing soil impoverishment. By the end of the Bronze Age, most of Shetland's pastoral and wilderness areas had probably been converted to heather dominated heathland, and blanket peat growth was widespread.

Climatic Deterioration

Climatic deterioration during the later Holocene has occurred throughout north-west Europe. It seems to have gained pace in many areas of Britain during the late fourth/early third millennium BP, and by the middle of the third millennium temperatures were some $2^{\circ}C$ lower on average than they had been in the sixth millennium, with storms and precipitation becoming more frequent (Lamb, 1988). Exposure to strong, salt-laden winds is a major growth-limiting factor for trees in Shetland, and an increase in the incidence of gales would have been detrimental for tree growth in the Islands. Loss of trees coupled with increased precipitation would also have favoured peat growth.

Deterioration in the climate and the soils would have had a detrimental effect on arable agriculture in Shetland, and by c. 3000 BP settlement patterns may have resembled those of today, with nucleation of settlements on the coasts close to the increasingly limited arable land, and use of the hills mainly for grazing. These ecological pressures of later prehistory may help to explain why the Iron Age period in Shetland is characterised by increased evidence for warfare, territoriality and the building of defensible farmsteads (brochs) (Fojut, 1986).

Further climatic changes during the historic period also seem to have had a role to play in Shetland's landscape history, perhaps most noticeably through their influence on settlement and land-use. Lamb (1988) records a mild phase of climate in Britain during the early centuries AD, followed by a cold period with storms, wetness and more severe winters, particularly between c. 550 AD and c. 800 AD. More evidence is needed from a wider range of sites before reliable generalisations can be made, but a spread of blanket peats over former farmland during the first millennium AD is evidenced at both the Scord of Brouster (Keith-Lucas, 1986) and Kebister (Butler, 1992). This may indicate that climatic deterioration at this time provided a renewed impetus to peat inception on soils which had resisted peat growth throughout the preceding millennia. At some sites manuring and drainage of arable land may have become the main factor preventing peat growth.

Subsequent warming during the ninth and tenth centuries AD marked the start of a period of notable warmth, known as the "Little Optimum", which lasted until around the thirteenth or fourteenth century and which must have provided generally favourable conditions for agriculture in Shetland. There is palynological evidence from Kebister for arable expansion at the site during the twelfth or thirteenth centuries, and for subsequent contraction of arable land sometime during the fifteenth or sixteenth century. As with most land-use change in the past, it is difficult to know to what extent these were responses to natural as opposed to cultural factors. Climatic deterioration from c. 1500 AD, and its effect on arable agriculture, is well attested from Britain (Parry, 1987; Lamb, 1988), and Bigelow (1985) has argued that an increasing emphasis on fishing in Shetland at this time was a response to increasingly unreliable harvests and livestock mortality brought about by the worsening weather which culminated in the "Little Ice Age" of the seventeenth and eighteenth centuries.

Conclusion

This paper has attempted to use the available pollen and associated environmental evidence from Shetland to describe how the climate, ecology and land-use of the Islands may have changed during the course of the Holocene, and to discuss how some of the natural and cultural influences on landscape change may have operated. There is good reason to accept that Shetland was to some extent destined to experience a natural retrogression from limited woodland on brown-earth soils to heathland on acidic, podsolised and peaty soils, on account of its geographical and geological setting. This process has, however, been accelerated and enhanced since 5000 BP by additional pressures from climatic deterioration, woodland clearance for agricultural settlement, and the grazing and burning of heathland. A more comprehensive network of pollen and charcoal profiles is needed to establish the pattern and timing of these changes, but the available evidence suggests that whilst there was considerable reduction of woodland during Neolithic times, the most far-reaching changes probably occurred during the Bronze Age. This seems to have been the main period of heathland development — a process which may have simultaneously encouraged, and been encouraged by, an emphasis on heath farming. By Later Bronze Age times the landscape of Shetland was probably already quite similar to that of today, with extensive areas of heather dominated moorland and little remaining woodland.

References

Bennett, K.D., Boreham, S., Sharp, M.J. and Switsur, V.R. (1992) Holocene history of environment, vegetation and human settlement on Catta Ness, Lunnasting, Shetland. *Journal of Ecology*, **80**, 241-273.

Bennett, K.D., Boreham, S., Hill, K., Packman, S., Sharp, M.J., Switsur, V.R. (1993) Holocene environmental history at Gunnister, north Mainland, Shetland. In *The Quaternary of Shetland, Field Guide*. Birnie, J., Gordon, J., Bennett, K., and Hall, A. (eds) Quaternary Research Association, London, 83-98..

Bigelow, G.F. (1985) Sandwick, Unst and late Norse Shetland economy. In Smith, B. (ed) *Shetland Archaeology*. The Shetland Times, Lerwick, 95-127.

Birks, H.J.B. (1986) Late-Quaternary biotic changes in terrestrial and lacustrine environments, with particular reference to north-west Europe. In Berglund, B.E. (ed) *Handbook of Holocene Palaeoecology and Palaeohydrology*. Wiley, 3-66.

Birnie, J. (1981) *Environmental Changes in Shetland Since the End of the Last Glaciation*. Unpublished PhD Thesis, University of Aberdeen.

Birnie, J.F. (1984) Report on pollen analysis and palaeoenvironmental interpretation in association with excavations at Scatness, S. Mainland and Breckin, Yell. *Unpublished report to AOC Ltd.*, Scotland.

Birnie, J.F. (1993) Garths Voe, Shetland. In *Quaternary of Scotland*. Gordon J.E. and Sutherland, D.G. (eds), London, Chapman and Hall.

Butler, S.B. (1992) *Archaeopalynology of Ancient Settlement at Kebister, Shetland Islands*. Unpublished PhD Thesis, University of Sheffield.

Edwards, K.J. and Moss, A.G. (1993) Pollen data from the Loch of Brunatwatt, West Mainland. In *The Quaternary of Shetland, Field Guide*. Birnie, J., Gordon, J., Bennett, K., and Hall, A. (eds) Quaternary Research Association, London, 126-129.

Fojut, N. (1986) *A Guide to Prehistoric and Viking Shetland*. The Shetland Times, Lerwick.

Hoppe, G. (1965) Submarine peat in the Shetland Islands. *Geografiska Annaler* 47a, 195-203.

Hulme, P.D. and Durno, S.E. (1980) A contribution to the phytogeography of Shetland. *New Phytologist* 84, 165-169.

Johansen, J. (1975) Pollen diagrams from the Shetland and Faroe Islands. *New Phytologist*, 75, 369-387.

Johansen, J. (1978) The age and introduction of *Plantago lanceolata* to the Shetland Islands. *Danmarks Geologiske Undersogelse* (Geological Survey of Denmark) Yearbook, 1976, 45-48.

Johansen, J. (1985) Studies in the vegetational history of the Faroe and Shetland Islands. *Annales Societatis Scientiarum Faeroensis, Supplementum XI*. Torshavn.

Kaland, P.E. (1986) The origin and management of Norwegian coastal heaths as reflected by pollen analysis. In Behre, K.E. (ed) *Anthropogenic Indicators in Pollen Diagrams*. A.A. Balkema, 19-36.

Keith-Lucas, M. (1986) Neolithic impact on vegetation and subsequent vegetational development at Scord of Brouster. In Whittle, A. et al. *Scord of Brouster. An Early Agricultural Settlement on Shetland*. Oxford University Committee for Archaeology Monograph, 9, 92-108.

Lamb, H.H. (1988) *Weather, Climate and Human Affairs*. Routledge.

Moore, P.D. (1988) The development of moorland and upland mires. In Jones, M. (ed) *Archaeology and the Flora of the British Isles*. Oxford University Committee for Archaeology monograph 14, 116-122.

Parry, M.L. (1978) *Climatic Change, Agriculture and Settlement*. Dawson, Folkestone.

Spence, D. (1979) *Shetland's Living Landscape*. A Study in Island Plant Ecology. The Thule Press, Lerwick.

Whittington, G. (1980) A sub-peat dyke on Shurton Hill, mainland, Shetland. *Proceedings of the Society of Antiquaries of Scotland*, 109, 30-35.

Whittington, G. and Edwards, K.J. (1993) Vegetation change on Papa Stour, Shetland, Scotland: a response to coastal evolution and human interference? *The Holocene*, 3,1, 54-62.

Whittle, A., Keith-Lucas, M., Milles, A., Noddle, B., Rees, S. and Romans, J.C.C. (1986) *Scord of Brouster. An early agricultural settlement on Shetland*. Oxford University Committee for Archaeology Monograph 9.

AN ARCHAEOLOGICAL SURVEY OF FAIR ISLE, SHETLAND

John Hunter

The archaeological survey of Fair Isle was instigated as part of a programme of sites and monuments recording which was carried out in the Northern Isles by the University of Bradford between 1981 and 1987. This programme was deliberately targeted at small island landscapes, usually uninhabited, for a number of reasons that have been detailed previously (Hunter 1984, 1). The two main underlying factors, however, are worth reiterating here: the first is the comparatively high state of monument preservation which results from a combination of relative inaccessibility, and the second is the natural boundary which an island landscape offers inside which ancient settlement infrastructure might be assumed. This latter factor has already been explored in some detail elsewhere, notably on West Burra (Hedges 1984), on Oronsay (Mellars 1987) and for a later period, on Faroe (Baldwin 1983).

Archaeological survey work is traditionally confined to monuments normally interpreted as being pre-1500 AD in origin but recent fieldwork in the Scapa Flow region of Orkney has also demonstrated the importance of recording post-medieval and modern remains within the overall survey framework (e.g. Hunter et al 1982). This was extended to the Fair Isle project resulting in a monuments record which covers the period from prehistory through to the Second World War and provides a strong basis from which future research strategies can be formulated for any given period of settlement evolution. This short paper is intended to give some idea of the types of monument identified within this broad period, and provides a useful complement to a more extensive review of the island and its archaeological implications (Hunter 1996).

Fair Isle lies roughly half-way between the Orkney and Shetland group of islands respectively, over 25 miles north of North Ronaldsay its nearest Orcadian neighbour. The land area of Fair Isle is barely eight square kilometres and, with the exception of the regions immediately adjacent to the North Haven where the modern slipway is located and to its predecessor at the south of the island, the coastline is inaccessible and jagged. The landscape itself divides conveniently into two zones (fig 2): to the north an unpopulated region of moorland and to the south a comparatively lower region of pasture which contains both the modern and the historically documented earlier settlement. The division is emphasised by a stone-built wall and by an earlier earthen boundary which runs parallel crossing the full width of the island from east to west. The survey pattern followed this simple zoning and was undertaken annually over four seasons between 1984 and 1987; two seasons being predominantly concerned with the moorland region (Hunter 1985 and 1987) and two with the "lowland" region (Hunter 1984 and 1986). Work took place during early spring in order to maximise the combination of a low sun

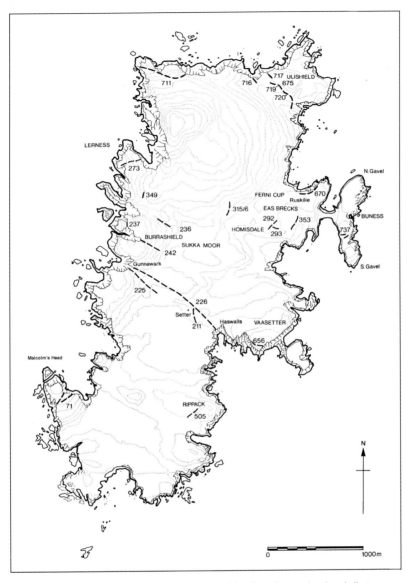

Fig 2. Outline of Fair Isle showing location of main surviving linear features (numbers indicate survey record).

13

and minimal vegetational growth. Survey was undertaken by close contact field walking and monuments were plotted using single station instrumentation. Detailed plans were made of the more important sites. The work was undertaken with generous support from the Russell Trust, the Shetland Amenity Trust and the Society of Antiquaries of Scotland. Generous assistance was also given by the owner of the island, the National Trust for Scotland, and by the Royal Commission on the Ancient and Historical Monuments of Scotland.

The creation of a sites and monuments record theoretically provides the database from which the landscape and settlement history can be evaluated, or at least interpreted. Here, for example, it provided the potential for identifying the changing face of long-term occupation on the island against a background of available economic resources and local subsistence activity. Survey is little more than the first step in assessing this information; archaeological investigation follows as a natural and logical exploratory tool. The picture is aided too by historical evidence, from Scandinavian influences starting from c AD 800, followed by Scottish influences from the 15th century and subsequently by more diverse factors. To be precise the historical evidence pertains to Shetland and it remains questionable as to whether it can accurately be applied to Fair Isle itself, an island both geographically and culturally peripheral. Certainly in later years the two could be considered synonymous; the main post-medieval changes that affected Shetland (i.e. land ownership and the fishing industry) affected Fair Isle too, and demonstrably so according to the historical evidence.

Much of Fair Isle's intrinsic archaeological value has been taken for granted "the only antiquity being a ring of loose stones 32 feet in diameter in the bottom of a hollow" (Muir 1885 76). Although no doubt using very different criteria the modern survey increased that number of identifiable monuments to around 750. Other sources, notably early maps, can be equally unhelpful and much of the cartographic evidence ignores the island either as being too small or too geographically separate to fit on the same map as Mainland Shetland. Foula suffers similar difficulties. Timothy Pont's 1630 map of Shetland places Fair Isle in the page margin, Seller's 1671 *English Pilot* merely locates its position and Kitchin's 1751 map manages to obscure it completely with a depiction of fishing scenes. Of all the early maps MacKenzie's *Orcades* (1752) alone covers it in any detail denoting a fairly accurate portrayal of the coastline, the main east-west earthen dyke that divides the island into two, and a small number of placenames. The placenames of Fair Isle deserve more attention than can be given here and their study relies heavily on a map of previously undocumented names gathered by a former warden at the island observatory. These include local landscape and field names still in use together with those remembered by older inhabitants which demonstrate a high, but not total, percentage of Scandinavian forms.

The analysis of an earlier population and its evolution is always helped by some understanding of the natural resources available to the population. On Fair Isle these resources seem to have been of limited attraction to the early settler and neither the geology nor the land use availability can be rated highly within the context of the Northern Isles as a whole. The geological basis of the island is of Old

Red Sandstone composed of sequences of sandstone and mudstone. Potential mineral resources might be derived from a number of dykes that cut the island allowing access to veins of sodic scapolite (Mykura and Young 1969) and copper ore. The former is not known to have been exploited but the latter has a modern documented history of investigation. Copper mining in Shetland was undertaken at a commercial level in the 19th and earlier 20th centuries and the few "copper" placenames on the island presumably date from this era. According to Mykura who investigated the deposits on Fair Isle in some detail, the veins were largely inaccessible. He describes earlier reports on their presence as being "exaggerated" (1972 43) and it seems unlikely that they were exploited to any great extent in antiquity. Other aspects of the local geology also seem to have been unrewarding, notably the availability of building materials. Fair Isle was not blessed with good building stone, nor for that matter even accessible stone from the steep cliffs, and this had major implications in interpreting the evolution of the landscape and settlement patterns. To some extent, therefore, the relevance of pursuing Scottish, Norse or Orcadian influences on the island becomes diminished if building traditions in those areas can neither be emulated nor developed on Fair Isle as a consequence of differences in structural materials.

One of the main natural resources available to society since the Iron Age has been peat, and Fair Isle is fortunate in having substantial deposits, albeit located in the least accessible part of the moorland landscape. The value of this fuel resource even in post-medieval times can be judged from the fact that the islanders of North Ronaldsay were regularly obliged to row 14 miles to Eday, their own nearest supply source. On Fair Isle peat transport was provided by ponies kept specifically for the purpose. Like ponies elsewhere in Shetland these were allowed to roam freely outside the hill dyke, even in winter, and this played its part in altering the vegetational history of the island.

The grazing of ponies, sheep, cattle and even pigs beyond the hill dyke has done much to change the original nature of the moorland vegetation throughout Shetland. Spence, working in the 1950s, successfully managed to identify patches of relic landscape in Shetland, mostly in the small islands of inland lochs where neither grazing nor burning had occurred (Spence 1960). Comparison of species derived from these and modern moorland respectively shows interesting differences which are now being amplified as the pollen records become established. Nevertheless, whatever vegetational changes occurred on Fair Isle they were not of sufficient magnitude to affect one of the island's major attractions and traditional resources, the bird population. Today Fair Isle houses one of the largest seabird colonies in Shetland, a fact which was no doubt an important subsistence asset to earlier peoples living on the island, especially bearing in mind the limited resources offered by the rest of the landscape. Bird remains from archaeological sites in Shetland have already been the subject of a preliminary analysis (Bourne and Dixon 1974) and in view of their importance and the number of sites now being excavated, an update would be a welcome addition to research literature.

Field research is frequently a limiting exercise which attempts to assess the significance of monuments whose forms are usually disguised by collapse and

Fig 3. The north-west end of a major boundary feature on Fair Isle. The large stones are all that remains of an original earth and turf covered feature.

vegetational cover. Dating tends to be by analogy and a fuller understanding can only normally be reached by means of archaeological investigation. One class of monument, however, which often closely resembles an original form is the linear feature and Fair Isle, like many other parts of the Northern Isles, contains a number of examples of varying types (fig 2). The largest of these is the great earthen "feelie" dyke with a maximum width of about 8m and surviving height of about 2m which runs across the island from Gunnawark to Heswalls. Similar monuments bisect the islands of Papa Stour, Foula and also Fetlar where, like Fair Isle, a later stone wall runs parallel. In each case they separate the hill land (scattald) from the farmland but whether this is a derived division based on an earlier boundary, similar for example to the "treb dyke" form of monument observed in Orkney, or a deliberate division of the landscape into two functional parts remains open to question. MacKenzie's chart which depicts the Fair Isle example in 1752 is the earliest record of its existence.

Elsewhere on the island linear features also appear to define headlands or areas of land which contain headlands. These are of smaller construction seemingly formed by aligning large stones at intervals across the landscape and then infilling the spaces with earth, turf and smaller stones (fig 3). Presumably this method of preventing access to a headland represents the most efficient way of creating an enclosure for livestock. It can be no co-incidence that local names such as *Hestaness* and *Buness* contain animal elements (hesta-horse; bu-cattle), although neither currently show any sign of enclosuring. Interestingly, however, a record in

16

the *Second Statistical Account* describes how the headland of Buness was "fenced off with a high stone dyke across its isthmus" (NSA 95).

Other linear forms may indeed contain an implicit territorial or boundary component, notably a pair of parallel features (at Burrashield) located within gullies and constructed in a manner which suggests that they were intrinsic to a group of over 20 turf-based structures of unknown date (see below) located in the land contained between them. One of the pair included a cairn as part of its alignment. Investigation of these related structures would doubtless shed some light on the antiquity of the boundaries themselves, which are notoriously difficult to date. Earthen land divisions are an attested facet of the Shetland landscape even in relatively modern times and traditional construction techniques survive well into the post-medieval period. John Walker, for example, in his later 18th century journey in the north described how the "fields were enclosed with walls of earth very broad at the foundations, five or six feet high and covered with grass from top to bottom" (cited in Shaw 1980 83). He added that they were "a constant bother to maintain". On the other hand boundaries of similar construction were seen during the survey in another part of the island in the sections of land drains where they occurred below the peat formation, suggesting a fairly early date. The problem lies in distinguishing features constructed at an early date from those which merely used an early, but ongoing constructional tradition.

One linear feature, identified over a distance of some 400m, not only isolated a series of headlands but also contained two structural forms as part of its length, apparently linked together along the boundary system. Both were sub-circular, of stone foundation construction and one, on superficial excavation, contained evidence of internal arrangements appropriate to a prehistoric burial cairn.

These linear features tend to occur in the marginal parts of the island, in those locations where agriculture and settlement changes have had minimal effect. In many areas where landuse has made a major impact, these features might be denoted as mere survivors from development, agricultural change and erosion. On Fair Isle, given the traditional foci of settlement and land use, one suspects that they represent an accurate tally rather then a residual sample. Some proof of this might be given by the plotted distribution of burnt mounds on the island. These monuments, of which 28 examples were recorded on Fair Isle (fig 4), on current thinking pertain to a process of domestic cooking activity (Hedges 1975 but also Buckley 1990) within the later Bronze Age and possibly the earlier Iron Age. The mounds are formed by the gradual accumulation of stones which have been fire-heated and then quenched to heat water. Re-use may occur but the form of the mound is often crescent-shaped which reflects a discard pattern as much as recent quarrying. Their domestic connotation implicitly assumes adjacent habitation and the mounds might therefore be used as a broad indicator of former settlement location. Their distribution on Fair Isle shows that survival is not confined to the margins or the moorland but occurs also on land which is currently under pasture, plough and modern activity.

Less substantial monuments will invariably be more vulnerable to destruction or erosion and therefore their survival in the moorland regions is seen as

17

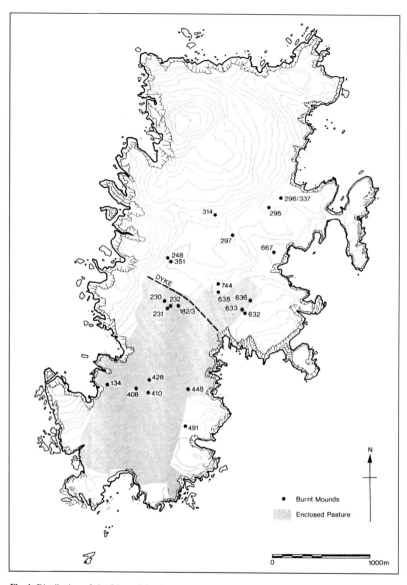

Fig 4. Distribution of the 24 surviving burnt mounds in both enclosed and moorland zones, Fair Isle (numbers indicate survey record).

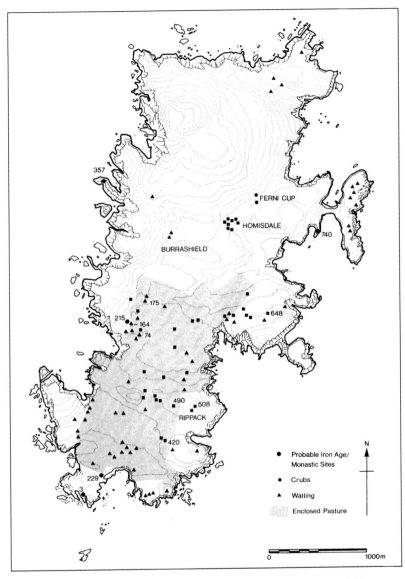

Fig 5. Distribution of surviving planticrubs and isolated walling lengths, Fair Isle (numbers indicate survey record).

a more selective phenomenon. In this respect one group of examples located in a moorland valley known as the "Ferni Cup" deserves special mention. The group represents a unit of relic landscape consisting of cairns, field boundaries, burnt mounds and, perhaps most important of all, associated structural remains. A dwelling house focal to the remains typifies the remarkable state of preservation of the moorland monuments on Fair Isle. Standing to a height of approximately 1m, it still exhibits internal arrangements, flooring and a number of associated features. The pattern of monuments seen here is arguably one originally repeated in all burnt mound locations recorded elsewhere on the island.

Not all structures, however, offer such relative ease of interpretation. Numerous less tangible forms were recorded during the survey and these will require reassessment subsequent to trial excavation. One group in particular, located at Burrashield to the west of the airstrip, consists of over 20 rectangular and sub-rectangular turf foundations often surviving no higher than approximately 30cm. These appear to have been specifically positioned in a terraced fashion against the base of a hillside and constructed roughly along the valley contour. There is some minor variation in format but many conform to dimensions of about 4 x 3m internally. A small number are stone-based and the group as a whole is defined to the north and the south by boundary dykes mentioned above. Interestingly, the group also includes a pair of burnt mounds.

Fundamental questions regarding function, date and constructional method are all open to wide speculation and the closest published parallels would seem to lie in south-west Scotland in the form of a group of platform dwellings (Corser 1982). Another, perhaps more realistic interpretation, sees them as a form of plantiecrub with a turf base and a palisade similar to a type previously illustrated by O'Dell (1939 78), but even this does not fully explain either their remote location or their apparent enclosing to the north and the south. Turf was a well attested building material in the Northern Isles as well as elsewhere in the N. Atlantic (Agustsson 1982) and the scattald system allowed for turf cutting as well as for peat cutting and grazing rights. In Fair Isle it was more easily obtainable than peat (or stone for that matter) but its building function was presumably in serious conflict with its primary grazing function. It is therefore surprising that other similar turf-based forms were identified in the vicinity of the present kirk in the traditional area of pasture in the south. Like examples elsewhere on the island the extent to which they may have been occupied on a permanent or temporary basis, or simply used as a planting out station for seedlings, awaits further archaeological comment.

Similar issues surround structural remains of a more substantial nature, namely the lengths of walling that litter both pasture and margins and which currently act as sheep shelters (fig 5). The post-medieval pasture economy of Fair Isle and other parts of Shetland have seen the development of a number of landscape features, normally built of stone, used specifically for the shelter, safety and herding of sheep (Baldwin 1978). On Fair Isle the forms vary from single straight lengths of about 5m to more complex H-shaped, L-shaped or Y-shaped designs of over 20m in length (fig 6). The common characteristic is that of stone construction, often with impressively large foundation and end stones. There can be

Fig 6. One of the short isolated lengths of walling which may often mark the site of an earlier structure.

little strength in the argument that they were purpose built for their current function; a more likely interpretation sees them as being recent modifications which utilised existing stone resources on an island where useful building stone is at a premium. As such it seems reasonable to assume that each walling unit represents the approximate vicinity of a previous, but now defunct, dwelling or settlement area and that a plot of their distribution may act as a guide to earlier settlement patterns. This hypothesis was tested by excavation in 1989 with promising results (Hunter 1996, ch 7).

The same interpretation can be applied to the distribution of planticrubs. These small square or sub-rectangular stone structures built to a typical height of around 1.5m, have much in common with the so-called sheep shelters: their distribution is varied both within and without the modern settled area, their constructional method is similar and they both lack any obvious spatial relationship or association with other structural forms or landscape features. It seems unreasonable to believe that the planticrub was a building that was locationally specific, otherwise we might expect to find it in more accessible places. Rather does it seem, as with the sheep shelters, that its distribution reflects the pattern of pre-existing structural remains.

Closer inspection of several of these crubs suggests that the evolved enclosure shape required for the growing of seedlings was certainly brought about by a secondary modification of the stonework. A number appear to exhibit obvious rebuilding, butted joints, blockings or other features indicative of structural

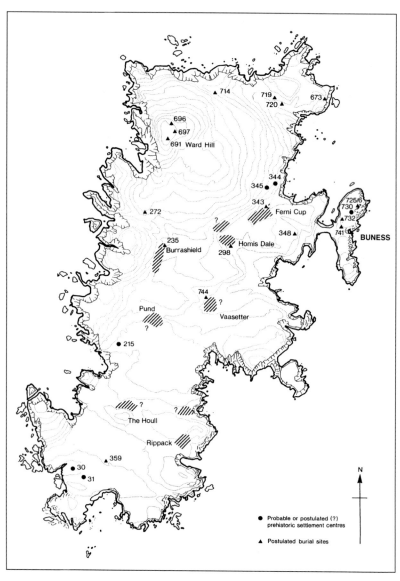

Fig 7. Probable early settlement centres according to distribution of planticrubs, walling, burnt mounds and linear earthworks, Fair Isle (numbers indicate survey record).

alteration to an existing form. One might include, in addition, the occurrence of a low grassy mound either totally or partially circumscribing the walling in a number of instances. One interpretation of this explains the mound as being the accumulation of organic deposits and soil removed from the interior of the crub, but it seems equally plausible that in some instances the mound may represent the remains of a pre-existing structure the stone of which was robbed in order to create a crub within the shelter of the former foundations. The location of the crub is therefore to some extent pre-determined by existing remains. A combination of crubs, walling lengths, burnt mounds and linear earthworks might therefore be used to identify the foci of early settlement (fig 7).

The identification of former dwellings would go some way to help explain the geography of settlement in various parts of the island, particularly in periods of population pressure and land shortage. In documented times a known peak occurred in the 1860s when the population stood at around 360, a figure roughly twice that noted by Low a century earlier (1774 196). Low's observations predate by only a generation the *First Statistical Account* entry of the late 18th century which points to the population living in "four clumps or towns" the names of which "Shewah", "Lioh", "Bustah" and "Gelah" are still identifiable (OSA 436). The survey was only able to identify concentrations of settlement remains around one of these, Shirva ("Shewah").

The earliest recorded reference to buildings on the island belongs to 1588 and to a description made by a sailor from *El Gran Grifon*, an Armada vessel wrecked on the south-east cliffs of Fair Isle. It relates how the island was peopled by 17 households living in huts (Ker 1920 172). By the time of the *Second Statistical Account* the number of households had more than doubled and outsets were being occupied (NSA 96). It seems clear from this and from the survey that individual, isolated dwellings were becoming commonplace and that while a pattern of nucleated settlement was dominant, it was by no means universal. The status and rights enjoyed by these individual units merit further study.

The locations of the "missing" dwellings implied by the peak population in the 19th century may partly be resolved by the distribution of sheep shelters and crubs, or even by the turf-based forms. Others may lie under modern houses according to a well attested process of locational continuity demonstrated elsewhere in Shetland (Small 1969). The constructional method may have differed little from Armada times and is a reflection of the limitations imposed by the natural materials available. Hibbert's 1822 description of crofts at Quendale (S. Mainland) might probably apply here. They were "built of rude stones, with a cement of clay, or they are, still more crudely formed of stones or clods" (1822 114f). Some insight too is given into the domestic arrangements which seem little different from those of Norse times the byre was usually adjoined to the dwelling and both were entered by a common door so that the visitor was introduced "first to the cattle and afterwards to the apartment devoted to the use of the family" (ibid).

Settlement patterning and land division are inseparable phenomena and successful attempts have been made, for example on Foula (Baldwin 1984), to extrapolate patterns of earlier settlement evolution from more recently recorded field divisions. These are less easily identifiable on Fair Isle, although maps resulting from the survey emphasise the anomalous alignments and widths of earlier and later rig lines respectively. Even by the mid-18th century the system of land tenure operating on Fair Isle was probably still Norse-derived and might be inferred from modern remains. A key component for this type of study is the placename evidence and although Fair Isle is bettered by Foula in terms of the physical survival of infield boundaries, it is no less endowed with placenames and there is considerable potential for future work in this quarter. Such a study, of course, rests on the premise that placename models of settlement evolution are in fact applicable and that, for example in the case of a Marwick-based model, it is fair to assume the presence of original dominant farmsteads in the Norse period. One might question too the justification of using an Orkney model, however workable it might prove to be in Orkney itself, in Shetland. Monteith, writing about Dunrossness, S. Mainland in 1845 and using an earlier source, pointed out that the inhabitants of that parish (which included Fair Isle at that time) were largely "strangers from Scotland and Orkney" who brought their own building techniques with them, notably the circular corn drier (1845 48f). It certainly seems true that in late medieval and historic times Orkney culturally looked southwards while Shetland had begun to look eastwards again. Given that Scottish influences are identifiable in Orkney and Norwegian influences are best seen in Shetland the problem of Fair Isle, lying neatly in between, becomes more emphatic.

A similar problem is encountered in attempting to assess the role and influence of the early church on Fair Isle. In Shetland the division and rationale behind the parish structure appears to be scattald-related and differs somewhat from that in Orkney where the Church organisation can be traced back to a urisland system. Exactly how Fair Isle fitted into either of these schemes, if indeed it conformed at all, is highly questionable partly because of its geographical position and partly due to a general absence of documentary and archaeological evidence.

Remarkably little survives from the earliest ingress of Christianity in Shetland although it seems likely that the primary motivation was supplied by the Columban missions. The layout and organisation of early monasticism, however, is still largely unresolved in the Northern Isles and it is difficult (if not impossible) to distinguish between a secular and an ecclesiastical community by archaeological means. The first recorded reference to Fair Isle is relatively late and refers to "St. Peter's Stouk" (Cant 1975 45, note) which implies a small outlying chapel dependent upon a larger benefice, presumably in Dunrossness, Mainland Shetland. Although Fair Isle spent a relative short period of time in the 18th century combined with Foula and Skerries as part of an unwieldy "islands" parish, it was to the parish of Dunrossness that it belonged for most of its recorded history and from where it received its Christian stimulus and administration. The present Kirk on the island is at a relatively new location but its predecessor, now removed apart from the graveyard, was situated at the south of the island at the head of Kirkgeo where conventional and geophysical survey have identified possible boundary walling. The structure that was demolished belonged to the 17th century although the site itself is probably somewhat earlier, a fact bourne out by the recovery of later Iron

Fig 8. The surviving remains of a horizontal-wheeled mill. The millstone lies in its original position.

Age pottery (N. Fojut *pers comm*) from salvage excavations at the eroding cliff edge. In addition to this site the placename *Kirkalees* adjacent to Shirva has traditionally been associated with a former church and burial ground.

More positive later structures, but with equally arguable ancestry, are the remains of the water mills whose stone foundations and part-standing walling can still be seen along the burn of Gilsetter at the east of the island (fig 8). They belong to a complicated systems of dykes, water coursing and drainage patterns which focus into a concentration of mill stations and dams as the burn flows out at Funniquoy. A maximum of nine such mills are recorded but the remains of only four are now visible and these have declined considerably since a photograph taken around 1916 (Waterson and Jones 1981 33).

The best two examples, Shirva Mill and New Mill, each show a superstructure of approximately 5 x 3.5m located over a race fed by (presumably moveable) lades. Their most important characteristic, however, is that they functioned by means of a horizontal wheel, a feature which they share with most other Shetland mills. The type is of restricted distribution and has been the subject of considerable interest, notably by Goudie who in his *Celtic and Scandinavian Antiquities of Shetland* described it as a type "so archaic as to be almost wholly unknown beyond its immediate area" (1904, 246). More modern scholarship (e.g. Wikander 1986) has shown that this distribution appears confined to Shetland (including some Orkney examples), Scandinavia, Ireland and parts of the Mediterranean. Its evolution, stemming from Roman times, has been variously interpreted but seems most suitably explained as belonging latterly to Viking influences. The date of the Fair Isle examples represents the final phase of this evolution but although the mills were still in use in the late 19th century the date of construction is uncertain.

Viking influences are also to be seen in aspects of the maritime environment which made an understandably significant impact on the island's history. The characteristic local boat, the Fair Isle yoal, stems from a Scandinavian design tradition and has been the subject of study within the context of the origin of Shetland boats generally (e.g. Ostler 1983 67-78). Although the pedigree is only indirect, being introduced from Norway in the 18th and 19th centuries, it seems reasonable to suppose that its presence marks the reappearance of a boat building evolution which was already in progress on Fair Isle in Viking times. This long-standing Norwegian tradition can also probably be extended to the associated boat-noosts, some of which are stone-lined, located at the south of the island. The most obvious examples lie where they divide into summer (lower) and winter (higher) types (fig 9), although the oldest remains, and those recorded in the *First Statistical Account* (OSA 436), are probably located a little further to the east below Gelah.

A combination of Fair Isle's jagged coastline, a location in dangerous waters between Orkney and Shetland and a pivotal position adjacent to the Atlantic shipping routes has made the island a notorious site for wrecks since historical records began. The most famous of these belongs to *El Gran Grifon*, an Armada supply ship, from which one stranded sailor describes the Fair Isle natives as being "savage people whose usual food is fish, without bread except a few barley meal

Fig 9. The group of boat noosts at Kirkgeo, showing both winter (upper) and summer (lower) noosts.

bannocks cooked over the embers of a fuel which they . . call turf" (Ker 1920 172). This account of 1588 bears witness to a poverty-stricken population concerned almost entirely with a seasonal subsistence economy divided between crofting and small scale fishing.

Fishing was later to play a more significant part in the economy of the island, particularly when the intense population pressures of the mid-19th century outgrew the available resources of the land. Until the end of the 18th century fishing appears to have been a relatively straightforward subsistence exercise which operated out of the south harbour which was appropriately situated adjacent to both the local fishing grounds and to the centres of population. It was an exercise that led to the development of trade with larger ships, exchanging feathers, fresh produce and woollens for items that were otherwise unobtainable on the island. This barter could occur many miles offshore and the activities of these "pitiful skiffs" (OSA 437) is almost a standard feature in the travel diaries of 18th and 19th century gentry (e.g. Low 1774 65; Schaw 1939 39).

By the end of the 18th century, however, Shetland had moved more heavily into the herring industry and the merchant lairds had created a situation which required more intensive "haaf" or deep sea fishing, often at the expense of the terrestrial economy. These involved changes of emphasis that necessitated, among other things, larger boats and larger crews neither of which Fair Isle seemed able to produce. What little evidence there is suggests that fishing operated more perilously (and on occasions more tragically) further afield and in deeper waters.

Archaeological traces of this activity survive only in the form of fish drying platforms — small expanses of beach stones laid out at convenient distances from the shore. Other evidence in the form of "skeo" names, identifying small purpose-built stone structures for fish-hanging, appear on Thomas' 1839 map of the island, although no physical remains were identified during the survey.

Finally, some mention must be made of the surviving military monuments which form a late but important (although arguably unsightly) part of the island's archaeological landscape. With the exception of the remains of a Napoleonic tower on the crest of Malcolm's Head at the west of the island, all the surviving monuments appear to belong to the 20th century, the majority clustering around Ward Hill the highest point on Fair Isle. This peak is traditionally the location of the Norse beacon used for signalling between Mainland Shetland and North Ronaldsay. The site is recorded in the Orkneyinga Saga as being integral to a plot around 1130 which resulted in the death of Dagfinn an inhabitant of Fair Isle (Palsson and Edwards 1978 119). Many of the military sites are represented by small earthworks, dugouts or terraces but more substantial monuments in the form of concrete structures, several of which are still roofed, line the eastern approaches to Ward Hill. Those on the skyline of the hill, the site of an important wartime radar station, have been razed and it is not possible by survey alone to identify individual forms from among the heaps of concrete rubble and metal which cover the hill top.

Elsewhere on the island one military site deserves special mention — the tailplane remains of a Heinkel aircraft which crash-landed on the island during a reconnaissance mission in 1941. The crew survived and wreckage of the plane can still be found throughout the surrounding fields. This tailplane, still largely intact, typifies the remarkable degree of preservation that Fair Isle exhibits from all periods of its past, from prehistory through to the age of aviation. There can be few other locations where this level of survival occurs so consistently and where it becomes possible to establish a sites and monuments database with such potential. Field survey is only the first step in the process of understanding man's past, but it provides the fundamental information necessary for subsequent historical research, archaeological excavation, heritage management and even tourism.

Postscript

This paper was originally written for delivery at the "Shetland Settlement" conference in 1988. Some elements of the research have been superceeded by recent study of the island.

References

Agustsson H. 1982, "Den indre opbygning af det islandke torvehus" in Myhre B. Stoklund B. and Gjaerder P. (eds) *Vestnordisk byggeskikk gjennom to tusen ar*, Arkeologisk Museum i Stavanger, Skrifter 7, 173-185

Baldwin J. R. 1978, "Norse influences in sheep husbandry on Foula, Shetland" in Baldwin J. R. (ed) *Scandinavian Shetland. An Ongoing Tradition* 97-127.

Baldwin J. R. 1983, "Structure in a community: the outfield, its use and its organisation in the settlement at Gasadalar, Faroe Islands", *Northern Studies* 20.

Baldwin J. R. 1984, "Hogin and Hametoun: Thoughts on the Stratification of a Foula *Tun*" in Crawford B. E. (ed) *Essays in Shetland History* 33-64.

Bourne W. R. P. and Dixon T. J. 1974, "The seabirds of Shetland" in Goodier R. (ed) *The Natural Environment of Shetland*, Nature Conservancy Council 130-144.

Buckley V. (ed) 1990, *Burnt Offerings*, Edinburgh.

Cant R. G. 1975, *The Medieval Churches and Chapels of Shetland*, Lerwick.

Corser P. 1982, "Platform buildings, Medieval settlements in Eskdale, Dumfriesshire", *Scottish Archaeological Review* 1, 1, 38-44.

Goudie G. 1904, *The Celtic and Scandinavian Antiquities of Shetland*, London and Edinburgh.

Heddle M. F. 1879, "The geognosy and mineralogy of Scotland. Mainland (Shetland), Foula, Fair Isle", *Mineralogy Mag* 3, 18-56.

Hedges J. 1975, "Excavation of two Orcadian burnt mounds", *Proc Soc Ant Scot* 106, (1974-5), 39-98.

Hedges J. 1984, "Gordon Parry's West Burra Survey", *Glasgow Archaeological Journal* 11, 41-59.

Hibbert S. 1822, *A Description of the Shetland Islands*, Edinburgh.

Hunter J. R., Dockrill S.J. and McKinley J.I. 1982, *The Sites and Monuments of Fara, Orkney*, BUSAS Occ Paper No. 1.

Hunter J. R. (ed) 1984, *Fair Isle Survey, Interim 1984*, BUSAS Occ Paper No. 5.

Hunter J. R. (ed) 1985, *Fair Isle Survey, Interim 1985*, BUSAS Occ Paper No. 6.

Hunter J. R. (ed) 1986, *Fair Isle Survey, Interim 1986*, BUSAS Occ Paper No. 7.

Hunter J. R. (ed) 1987, *Fair Isle Survey, Interim 1987*, BUSAS Occ Paper No. 8.

Hunter J. R. 1996, *Fair Isle: The Archaeology of an Island Community*, H.M.S.O. and the National Trust for Scotland, Edinburgh.

Ker W. P. 1920, "The Spanish Story of the Armada", *Scottish Historical Review* 17:67, 165-176.

Low G. 1774 (1879), *A Tour Through the Islands of Orkney and Schetland*.

MacKenzie M. 1752, *Orcades: or a geographic and hydrographic survey of Orkney and Lewis islands*, Edinburgh.

Mellars P. 1987, *Excavations in Oronsay*, Edinburgh.

Monteith R. 1845, *Description of the islands of Orkney and Zetland 1633*, Edinburgh.

Muir T.S. 1885, *Ecclesiological Notes on Some of the Islands of Scotland*, Edinburgh.

Mykura W., 1972, "Igneous intrusions and mineralisations in Fair Isle, Shetland Islands", *Bull Geol Surv Gt Br 41*, 33-53.

Mykura W. and Young B. R. 1969, "Sodic scapolite (dipyre) in the Shetland Islands", *Rpt Inst Geol Sci* 69/4.

NSA (1845), *New Statistical Account of Scotland*, Vol XV, Sutherland, Caithness, Orkney, Shetland — General Index, Edinburgh and London.

O'Dell A.C. 1939, *The Historical Geography of the Shetland Islands*, Lerwick.

OSA (1978), Sinclair Sir John (ed) *The Statistical Account of Scotland 1791 - 1799*, Vol XIX, *Orkney and Shetland*. Facsimile edition, Thomson W. P. L. and Graham J. J. (eds), Wakefield

Ostler A.G. 1983, *The Shetland Boat, South Mainland and Fair Isle*. National Maritime Museum Monograph and Reports No. 58.

Palsson H. and Edwards P. (eds) 1978, *Orkneyinga Saga*, London.

Schaw J. 1939, *Journal of a lady of quality; being the narrative of a journey from Scotland to the West Indies, North Carolina and Portugal, in the years 1774 to 1776* (Andrews E. W. ed) Yale.

Shaw F.J. 1980, *The Northern and Western Isles of Scotland*, Edinburgh.

Small A. 1969, "The distribution of settlement in Shetland and Faroe in Viking times", *Saga Book* 17, 2-3, 144-155.

Spence D. H. N. 1960, "Studies in the vegetation of Shetland III. Scrub vegetation of Shetland and S Uist", *J Ecol* 48, 73-95.

Thomas G. 1839, *Chart of the Shetland Islands*, London.

Waterson G. and Jones J. 1981, *Fair Isle, a photographic history*, Edinburgh.

Widander O. 1986, "Archaeological evidence for early watermills — an interim report" in Smith N. (ed) *History of Technology* 10, 151-180.

BUSAS = Bradford University School of Archaeological Sciences.

FROM PAST TO PRESENT AT KEBISTER

UNFOLDING THE STORY OF ONE SHETLAND FARM

Olwyn Owen

At first sight, the deserted farm of Kebister appears a rather unremarkable place. It is located on the south side of Dales Voe just north of Lerwick (fig 10), and mainly comprises an undulating, peat-covered hillside, which rises from sea level to a shelf of about 70m over datum. This shelf is bounded by the Hill of Gremista to the south and a prominent peak, Luggie's Knowe, to the north-east. At the foot of the slope, a grass-covered strip cropped by grazing sheep borders the rocky coastline. A closer look reveals a cluster of ruinous crofts, known locally as Handigarth (W. and M. Anderson, pers comm), which are situated towards the top edge of the grassy strip. They lie adjacent to the Burn of Kebister, a perennial stream which, fed from the peat slopes above, flows down the hillside and into the Voe. Today, Kebister is dominated by the new oil rig supply base with its access road, whose construction in 1985/86 prompted Historic Scotland (then, SDD-HBM) to commission an archaeological investigation.

As in so many parts of Shetland, the boggy, heather-covered hillside at Kebister masks most traces of its long and varied past; and it was only on the grass-covered coastal strip that archaeological remains could be clearly detected before excavation. The turf-covered outline of a large, rectangular building and a number of small, enigmatic mounds immediately adjacent to it formed the subjects of the initial excavations in 1985, for these were directly in the line of the then proposed development.

Between 1985-87, the archaeological team spent a total of almost eight months at Kebister and excavated an area of approximately 900 square metres. Excavation revealed a series of fragmentary structures and associated deposits which appear to range in date from at least the Early Bronze Age to the Post-Medieval period. In short, those initially unpromising-looking mounds in fact marked the site of a multi-period farming settlement.

It is not the intention of this paper to report in detail on the excavated site; interim statements with illustrations are available elsewhere (Owen 1985; Owen and Lowe 1986; Owen 1987, Owen and Smith, 1985), and the full results will be submitted to the Society of Antiquaries of Scotland later this year (1996) for publication as a monograph. However, amongst the prehistoric structures, the following are particularly notable:

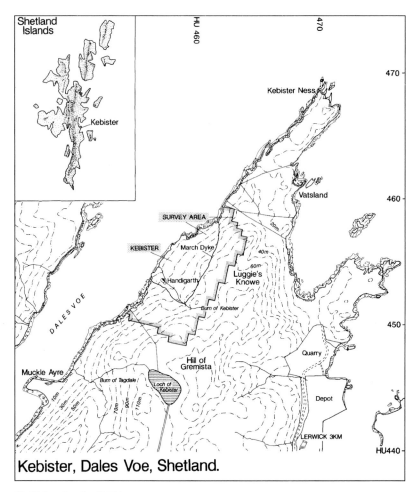

Kebister, Dales Voe, Shetland.

Fig 10. Location plan, Kebister.

Structure 1 A sub-rectangular building probably of the second millennium BC, its outline marked by a double ring of post-holes which once housed substantial timbers. The building had maximum dimensions of 7m by 5.2m and contained a large rectangular central hearth with a paved base and two large cooking pits;

Structure 3 An Iron Age house of which only about half survived. This sub-circular or D-shaped structure was built in the late first millennium BC and continued in use through several hundred years, well into the first millennium AD. A well-stratified sequence of superimposed floors, hearths and other deposits testify to this lengthy period of occupation. The building underwent major structural alterations during its lifetime and was extended at least once. The house was enclosed by a curvilinear yard where industrial and other activities took place;

Structure 4 An oval-shaped Iron Age house, constructed in the late first millennium BC and abandoned in the early first millennium AD (before Structure 3), and altered structurally at least once during its lifetime. It had massive walls of stone and turf but its maximum internal diameter was c4m. Its internal wall faces were punctuated by orthostats and interior recesses were built into the walls. This building also contained well-stratified occupation deposits; and

Structure 5 A sub-oval, cellular Iron Age building, erected probably at the very end of the first millennium BC or early in the first millennium AD. It had single-faced stone walls and measured at least 5.5 by 2.75m internally. It had more than one phase of construction and a series of reasonably well-preserved occupation levels survived. At one level, a paved floor of large slabs was laid throughout the interior.

Amongst the features associated with these and other fragmentary structures, at various times, were the following:

a)   an extensive deposit of prehistoric ploughsoil, up to 0.25m deep, scored and underlain by ardmarks (lines visible in the undisturbed sub-soil, created by a prehistoric plough or ard);

b)   repeated attempts to improve the drainage of the settlement site by the installation of gullies and stone-lined drains;

c)   areas studded with circular pits which served a variety of functions;

d)   an area covered with the flaked debris of sandstone knapping to produce crude stone implements.

From the Early Medieval period, the following features are of particular interest:

1)   a small rectangular structure, c6 by 3m in size, interpreted as a probable chapel. Its shape was outlined by slots cut into natural clay, and it was aligned east to west.

Two, much decayed, wooden coffins also aligned east to west, lay outside its eastern end. Wood from the coffins was radiocarbon dated to the tenth century (Norse period);

2)   a substantial heap of midden material located downslope of the probable chapel, which contained Norse and Medieval artefacts;

3) several fragments of stone structures which were probably Medieval, poorly preserved and square or rectangular. Unfortunately, few deposits associated with these structures survived.

The placename 'Kebister' is itself Norse, its first element perhaps deriving from the Shetland dialect word for a rowlock, 'kabe' (O.N. *keipr*), as Luggie's Knowe on the horizon, with the low hill-line on either side of it, resembles the rowlock of a boat when Kebister is approached from the sea (R. Leask, pers comm). This suggestion is strengthened by the fact that Luggie's Knowe was also called 'Da Kebb' (Jakobsen, 1928-32). The second element appears to derive from O.N. *bústaðr*, meaning a farm distantly created from an older parent farm (L. MacGregor, pers comm).

These traces of Norse and Medieval structures were, in turn, overlain by a substantial and rather fine, early sixteenth century building (the building first identified as under threat from the proposed development), which is now known to have been the teind bard of Archdeacon Henry Phankouth (1501-29) (Owen and Smith, 1988).

The site as a whole was rich in complete and fragmentary artefacts of durable materials such as stone, pottery and industrial waste, and, from the later periods, also glass, clay pipe and metalwork. Some 1,000 coarse stone artefacts were recovered, together with many hundreds of flakes from their manufacture (A. Clark, pers comm). Additionally, about 500 steatite artefacts or fragments thereof, over 1,000 pieces of worked quartz, about 50 pieces of pumice, approximately 4,000 sherds of pottery, and a large collection of other miscellaneous finds were retrieved.

The excavated prehistoric and early Medieval settlement represents repeated (rather than continuous) occupation of the same site and was clearly the nucleus of several episodes of probable subsistence farming at Kebister which, on present evidence, may span over 4,000 years. The soil is acidic and does not preserve shells or bone (other than small burnt fragments), which has inhibited reconstruction of the economy of the phases of the settlement. Nevertheless, the excavated materials do include evidence of its enduring agricultural basis. For instance, among the stone artefacts, several hundred flaked sandstone bars (perhaps used to break up the soil), stone ard points and quern stones and rubbers are indicative of cultivation and the on-site conversion of agricultural produce into foodstuffs. Analyses of fossil pollen grains, carbonised cereal grains, other macroplant remains, animal dung retrieved from samples or soil deposits both within and surrounding the domestic structures, and of the residues on cooking vessel sherds of pottery and steatite, are augmenting this picture of a subsistence-based farming economy.

A considerably fuller reconstruction of life in Post-Medieval Kebister is possible, partly because it is supported by historical documentation and partly because its basis is more immediately self-evident in the present day landscape. The seat of Post-Medieval (and perhaps Medieval) Kebister is at Handigarth, a farm-name probably deriving from O.N. *hangðagarðr*, meaning farm near or under a steep hill (B. Smith, pers. comm). Handigarth is situated approximately 100m

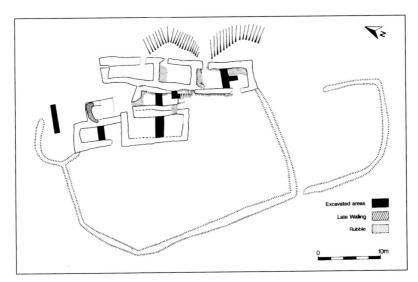

Fig 11. Farm at Handigarth, Kebister.

upslope and south-east of the excavated settlement, south of the Burn of Kebister (fig 10). In its final form, it comprised seven conjoined, rectangular structures built of rough drystone walling, all aligned north-west to south-east (fig 11). Two phases of adjoining rectangular enclosures are clearly visible. Traces of a water mill and race occur in the Burn adjacent to the settlement.

In the Post-Medieval period, once Phankouth's teind barn had fallen into disuse, probably by the mid sixteenth century, Kebister seems to have reverted to being a typical Shetland scattald (or settlement unit) (Smith 1984). Like all scattalds, it contained all those resources necessary for a comparatively self-contained economy. The local environment has not changed much over the intervening period. Then, as now, the site gave access to the sea along Dales Voe: although the shore is rocky, there were at least two boat-shelters (Nelson 1955), testifying to water-borne communications and to the possibility of sea fishing, even if only on a small scale. An area of hard-won arable and meadow land stretched back up the hill on the north-facing slope and was dotted with clearance cairns, field drains and small fields. Beyond, there was rough grazing for sheep, cattle and ponies, where peats could also be cut for fuel and turves for roofing. The Burn of Kebister provided fresh water and power for the small mill; while beyond the March Dyke which encircled the township was the rough pasture land with plenty of peats and fresh-water fishing in the Loch of Kebister. Kebister also had grazing rights to the Green Holm, a small island with pasture for a few sheep, while some of Kebister's cultivated land may have been at Vatsland, an area of lush pasture to the north-east (SRO, RS47/1, 55 et seq).

Surviving documents allow the identification of individual tenants at Kebister as early as the sixteenth century. Kebister was originally part of the

35

archdeaconry estate but it is likely that it gradually fell into secular hands after the Reformation. In 1577, "Stephanus of Kebustare" was one of 700 or so complainants against a tyrannical administrator of the islands (Balfour 1859, 17); and in 1639, both 'andro in kebusta' and 'adam taite' are listed as tax-payers there (SRO, GD190/box 33). More complete documentation exists for the eighteenth and nineteenth centuries, during which Kebister survived both famines and epidemics. In 1717, there was only one tenant paying tax at Kebister, James Sinclair (SRO, RH9/15/176, 28). During the late eighteenth century, as elsewhere in Shetland, the population increased, until in 1802 there were 15 inhabitants (SA D11/179). The last child to be born at Kebister was Agnes Morrison, in July 1817 (SRO, Tingwall OPR). Shortly afterwards the remaining inhabitants were removed to make space for a sheep farm. Kebister was the earliest Shetland township to be permanently 'cleared' in this way: its early abandonment has contributed to the good preservation of the archaeological record.

The records of Kebister's tax and rent assessments are informative about the status of the farm. When a qualitative land assessment was introduced on individual farms within each scattald, possibly as early as the twelfth or early thirteenth century, Kebister was assessed at 12 merks of arable land which is slightly lower than average for Shetland (SRO, RH9/15/176, 28). Later, Kebister's 12 merks were assessed at 8d the merk, again an average assessment (SRO, RS47/1, 55 et seq). There is, however, evidence that Kebister remained a single or, at most, a double household township until the early eighteenth century (SRO, RH9/15/176). Whereas other scattalds paid much higher tax, and other farms had much higher merk assessments, these scattalds often contained several farms and individual farms came to include several crofts. Kebister, with 12 merks for just one or two families, was probably a respectable holding. In 1777, the agent to Lord Dundas wrote of Litlaland, Fetlar, which has an exposed location on poor soil and, like Kebister, was assessed at 12 merks: "yet it happens here as almost everywhere in Shetland, that the sole tenant of the town by superior industry lives better and pays his rent more punctually than those that possess so much better land....where many tenants are crowded together and labour run rigg. For it holds universally, the more extensive the town and the more farmers upon it, the poorer they are" (SRO, RH4/102). Kebister probably escaped sub-division because it was just too small to support more than one or two households. Consequently, when lean times came, it was able to survive more easily than areas of better land which supported several families.

A document of 1722 detailing the real rents and teinds of townships in Tingwall parish (including Kebister) offers a fuller picture of Kebister's status as farmland (SA D.6/172). The figures for teinds indicate what each township was deemed able to pay in different commodities. Analysis of this record suggests that Kebister had a good pasture but that fishing was of negligible importance (B. Smith, pers comm). Of the 53 townships in Tingwall parish, Kebister is seventeenth highest overall in terms of the amount of money paid per merk. This is a good indication that, in the Post-Medieval period at least, Kebister was significantly above average within the parish in terms of its agricultural productivity.

The crofts at Handigarth are the most tangible remains of the Post-Medieval farm; similarly, the several excavated prehistoric structures represent the nucleus of the farming settlement in ancient times. They also have to be evaluated in terms of their environment, but this time in the absence of supporting documentary evidence and against a background of several thousand years of landscape evolution. For what determines the viability or otherwise of a settlement is the way in which people both interact with, and adapt to, the local environment. In a relatively self-contained economy such as this, settlement of any period is only as sustainable as the surrounding landscape is, or can be made to be, productive. The surviving structures and their contents reflect both the types of activities undertaken on the farmstead and the success or otherwise of one or all of those activities.

The productivity of a given landscape is finite, limited by a combination of natural and human factors. Natural limitations include such factors as climate, types of soil, steepness and aspect of slopes, proximity to water and availability of natural resources, such as suitable building materials. Human limitations might be summarised under the headings of human industry and ingenuity, by which means soils may (or may not, as the case may be) be improved, fields cleared and drained, pastures enclosed, efficiency increased, appropriate technology applied, available resources utilised and so forth.

In the case of Post-Medieval Kebister, the potential of a marginal agricultural site appears to have been maximised; the resources were assiduously exploited and the precarious balance between population numbers, landscape potential and human endeavour was sustained. Some attributes of this relatively self-contained, relatively successful, Post-Medieval farm are equally applicable to earlier farms on the same spot. For instance, its siting, near the centre of Shetland Mainland and on a navigable waterway, was probably as advantageous to the prehistoric inhabitants of Kebister as it was to the Post-Medieval community. In addition, the scale and number of excavated prehistoric structures suggest that, at any one time, as in the Post-Medieval period, the farmstead probably only supported one or two households. The overall picture of Post-Medieval Kebister cannot, however, be imposed directly and entirely on to prehistory because the landscape itself is not static.

Landscapes change, usually gradually, over the course of millennia. The process of change in Shetland can be taken to begin in the post-glacial period and continue up to the present day. During this period, local topography may have undergone radical change, from both natural processes and from the impact on the landscape of human activities. Natural changes include, for example, the gradual deterioration in climate over the past 3,500 years with its inevitable consequences, such as the formation, onset and spread of blanket peat. Human activities have included generations of manuring of the soil, or, on a shorter time-scale, quarrying for stone, to give but one example.

Some topographical changes happen quite quickly; others may take hundreds of years. Some changes, such as quarrying for stone, may in themselves be destructive of earlier archaeology; others, such as the encroachment of blanket peat, may preserve underlying archaeology but, in the process, may conceal it.

Archaeologically, the changes are of variable significance and, depending on the mechanisms which produced them, they may affect all or part of the landscape under study. Thus, the present day topography is a mosaic of topographical features of varying age. The oldest features, such as hilltops and lakes, may have survived from the pre-glacial period; the youngest features at Kebister are the new oil rig supply base and its access road. The challenge for the archaeologist is to unravel the history of a changing landscape, of which the archaeology is a part; for people are capable both of responding to and provoking change.

During the 1987 fieldwork at Kebister, we moved outwards from the excavated prehistoric settlement site and from Handigarth, the nucleus of the Post-Medieval farm, to encompass the whole hillside in a detailed survey. The initial aim was to reconstruct, as far as possible, the multi-faceted history of the landscape. Ultimately, it was hoped to place the separate phases of prehistoric occupation in their broader environmental contexts.

The intensive topographical survey method employed at Kebister was first developed at Machrie North, Arran in the late 1970s (Barber 1982; Barber forthcoming). It was refined subsequently on projects run from the, then, Scottish Central Excavation Unit in several areas of upland Scotland.

At Kebister, the area selected for survey extended roughly 1 kilometre along the coastline, centred on the excavation site, and stretched some 500m up the hillside. The natural topography provided some obvious boundaries to the area and, in this respect, being physically relatively self-contained, Kebister proved particularly well suited to this type of fieldwork. The area ran from Luggie's Knowe in the north-west to the foot of the Hill of Gremista in the south-east, and included most of the catchment area of the Burn of Kebister (fig 10).

As an essential reference framework, a grid was laid out over the hillside, the 50m intersections marked by bamboo canes labelled with grid co-ordinates. This produced over 200 squares of 50m by 50m, which were grouped into blocks of 5 by 5 squares (250 squares or parts thereof) (fig 12). Each 50m square was walked along transects at 5m intervals. The surveyors used prepared sheets to record all surface irregularities of greater than about 0.1m. Agreed conventions were used to record features (stones or groups of stones, mounds, dykes, fences, changes or breaks in slope, field drains, gullies, rigs, tracks and paths, streams, springs, water seepages, etc.). Peat depth was measured at the south-west corner of each 50m square and major variations in vegetation cover were noted (heather, rush, moss or grass). All the individual 50m squares were then collated into their blocks, which allowed linear and other large and/or fragmented features to be identified. Each block plan was subsequently checked with a repeat field visit, areas of potential archaeological interest probed and the block plans annotated accordingly.

For survey purposes, a monument was defined as any site where the effects of past human activity were discernible. At this stage, all monuments were given equal value, whether a prehistoric house or a tenuous clearance cairn. This is a necessary assumption at survey level, the relative values of monuments being considered later. Detailed recording of newly discovered monuments was undertaken as a separate exercise subsequent to the topographical survey; emphasis

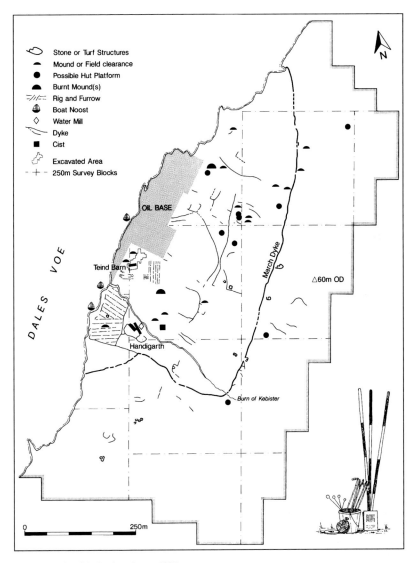

Fig 12. Results of the Kebister Survey 1987.

being placed on the relationships between adjacent monuments, where such existed.

Analysis of the Kebister survey data is continuing, and the results outlined below are provisional. Significantly, the topographical survey detected archaeological features on almost every bump and knoll on the hillside (fig 12). These ranged from cairns, through to fish or seaweed-drying walls, small cists and burnt mounds. A number of pre-peat and other turf-built dykes had been noted previously, but these increased markedly in number after topographical survey, giving a complex picture of millennia of land use and management. Several more-probable prehistoric house sites and several scattered turf-built enclosures were discovered, some of the latter probably plantiecrubs. Field edges, clearance cairns and square and rectangular fields with rigs were also recorded. Altogether, monuments were recorded at the rate of about 350 per square kilometre, where only a handful were known before.

Three archaeological sites of especial significance were located, besides that which has been excavated. Firstly, about 290m north-east of the excavated site, there is an area containing a concentration of at least six burnt mounds, adjacent to a dried-up stream bed (fig 13a). A large pre-peat dyke, which was traced over a total length of some 230m, runs above the scatter of burnt mounds. Immediately

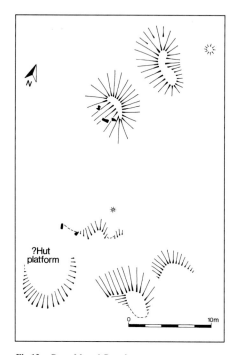

Fig 13a. Burnt Mound Complex.

40

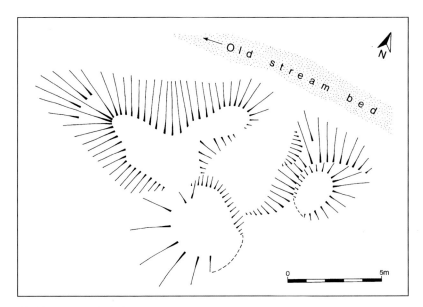

Fig 13b. Burnt mound, Kebister.

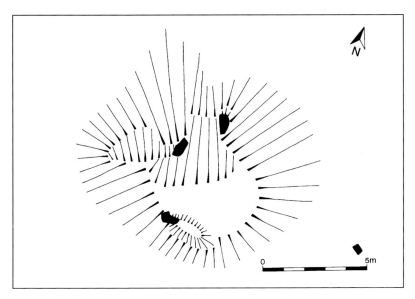

Fig 13c. Prehistoric house, Kebister.

41

above that, there are several cut platforms, tentatively identified as hut platform sites.

Secondly, a substantial, kidney-shaped burnt mound, 13m across, was located approximately 75m south-east of the excavation (fig 13b). It is situated adjacent to a dried-up stream bed and has a central depression which may well contain a cooking place (cf Hedges 1974-5).

Thirdly, another probable prehistoric house site was identified below Handigarth (fig 13c). It survives as a large mound, 11.5 by 10m across, and stands up to 1.5m high, but it has been flattened by cultivation on its eastern side. Some protruding stonework is visible, including possible orthostats.

The topographical survey was undertaken in tandem with other specialist surveys: soils, pollen and botany. These complemented the topographical survey in the field, but all results are being integrated in the post-survey analyses of the field data. At Kebister, a soil scientist, a pollen analyst and a botanist were present on site to supervise these aspects of the fieldwork. They worked to the same grid as the topographical surveyors, and were aided, during the preparatory stages and in the field, by the detailed study of large scale aerial photographs of the area.

For the soils, a land facet map, produced in advance from study of the aerial photographs, was refined during fieldwork. An initial, random soils survey was complemented by a gridded soils survey, during which the profiles of soil pits were recorded at every 100m grid intersection where the peat was less than 1m deep. A detailed soils map was thus produced, against which the essential characteristics of natural and anthropogenically influenced soils could be defined and the land use capability assessed. One of the most interesting and immediate findings from the gridded survey was the identification of a possible prehistoric cultivation horizon buried beneath up to 0.6m of peat (D. Jordan, pers comm).

Chemical analyses of soil samples are being undertaken to see if changes of activity can be ascertained on either side of several of the major dykes. High concentrations of phosphates, which can indicate areas of past manuring and other activities, can be mapped like contours. Additionally, the hypothesis that the Kebister soils are enriched by the presence of a small outcrop of gritty limestone in the immediate vicinity, is being tested. If correct, this might account for the preference for this area for settlement over the centuries. Of course, the presence of an earlier farm itself can contribute to soils enrichment, and increases the likelihood of later settlement in the same location.

The depth of the peat was measured by the topographical surveyors, using peat probes at every 50m intersection. The variability of peat depths was also tested by measuring depths along a selected transect of the area at 10m intervals. A map of the sub-surface topography was then produced. By dating the base of the peat at appropriate locations on the hillside, the encroachment of blanket peat down the hillside can be mapped chronologically. This information is used to indicate the approximate dates when areas at given heights above sea level became peat-covered and, therefore, unsuitable for agriculture or settlement. Peat depths analysis also shows areas where early monuments could not be discerned even by this intensive survey method because of the depth of peat grown over them. In conjunction with the topographical survey and analysis of selected pollen cores, it can indicate areas where peat cutting at different periods has been prevalent.

Regional and local peat cores were collected for subsequent pollen analysis to enable a broad reconstruction of the vegetation of past environments. A column of peat is effectively a slice through time, and analysis of the types of pollen preserved at different depths shows how the environment has changed over time. The regional core at Kebister, which was just under 3m deep, was taken from a peat-filled basin on the hilltop, approximately 500m from the excavated site, at a height of about 70m over sea level. Pollen analysis has shown that *Plantago lanceolata*, sometimes an indicator of the establishment of grazing pasture, first appeared at Kebister in the Neolithic period, between 2750 and 2400 bc (S. Butler, pers comm). There is a significant peak in its appearance between 2250 and 2000 bc.

The vegetation survey involved mapping, describing and quantifying the various plant communities present within the gridded area. This was done from aerial photographs initially, then refined in the field by collation of the topographical surveyors' records of major vegetation boundaries, supported by a detailed survey by a botanist of a structured sample of more than 200, 1 by 1m square quadrats. Such work can highlight areas of differential drainage and localised variations, indicative of underlying archaeology. Analysis of this data in conjunction with analysis of samples of present day surface pollen will show the extent to which modern pollen rain is representative of the vegetation of the area, as an aid to interpretation of ancient pollen spectra.

Overall this survey technique provides an extraordinarily detailed picture of the hillside and gives a new and much more rounded perspective to the excavated settlement site.

At the start of this paper, it was suggested that, at first sight, Kebister appears an unremarkable place. It is a salutary lesson indeed to recall how inauspicious those small amorphous mounds appeared at the outset of the project, and how few features were observed on our first excursions over the hillside. Had it not been for the size and intriguing nature of the Post-Medieval building first noted, and the Norse placename which suggested that a Viking farm might underlie it, the site might never have been excavated. The coincidental discovery of the prehistoric settlement immediately adjacent prompted the programme of intensive fieldwork which, in turn, revealed a complex pattern of prehistoric settlement and farming on the hillside at Kebister. It is probable that Kebister is not so uncommon after all. The continuing survey work of the Shetland archaeologist, Val Turner, may indeed prove that Kebister is an unremarkable place, through the discovery that much of Shetland's settlement is multi-period.

The substantial building originally threatened by the development represents an unusual episode in the long and fascinating life of this Shetland farm. In 1986, an elaborately carved armorial stone was discovered lying face down immediately outside the sole entrance to the building (fig 14). Originally it had been inserted into the wall above the door and lay where it had collapsed as the building decayed. The arms are almost certainly those of Henry Phankouth, a shadowy historical

Fig 14. Armorial Stone, Kebister.

figure who was archdeacon of Shetland from 1501-29; and the building they adorned was probably a collecting point and temporary store for teinds (tithes) and rents delivered to the archdeacon in kind (Owen and Smith 1988; Smith 1989). The Latin inscription on the stone reads like an epitaph to all those ancient settlements, and to all the people who have toiled on this hillside over thousands of years: *sine paulusper*, "Allow me [to remain] for a little while".

Acknowledgements

The Kebister project has relied on the work of many archaeologists, specialists and volunteers, too numerous to mention, but to all of whom I extend my thanks. In particular, I wish to thank Dr Christopher Lowe, co-director of the project, and David Jordan (soil science), Simon Butler (pollen analyst), Sandra Nye (botanist) and Ann Clark (stone artefacts), whose work in the field, and subsequently has provided some of the material for this paper. Brian Smith has been unstinting in his efforts to identify the owner of the armorial stone and to trace both Phankouth's origins and the history of Kebister; it is thanks to him that I have been able to present the documentary evidence for Post-Medieval Kebister here. Willy and Mary Anderson and Robert Leask provided valuable local information.

I am indebted to John Barber and Magnar Dalland for many discussions of the theoretical aspects of topographical survey.

The wholehearted co-operation of Lerwick Harbour Trust and the site developers is gratefully acknowledged; as is the help and kindness we received from individual Shetlanders, again too numerous to mention, throughout our work at Kebister. The project was funded by Historic Scotland, with contributions from Lerwick Harbour Trust and Shetland Amenity Trust.

The illustrations were drawn by Keith Speller (fig 10, 12, 13) and Sylvia Stevenson (fig 11); and the photograph (fig 14) was taken by Michael Brooks.

Postscript

This paper was originally written for delivery at the "Shetland Settlement" conference held in 1985. Since then some of the conclusions presented have been superseded. These will be presented in the final Kebister report, which is now in press.

References

Balfour, D (ed.) 1859 *Oppressions in the Islands of Orkney and Zetland*, Edinburgh

Barber, J 1982 'Arran', *Curr Archaeol*, 7 (1982), 358-63

Barber, J forthcoming *Arran 1978-81*, AOC (Scotland) Ltd. Monograph

Central Excavation Unit and Ancient Monuments Laboratory Annual Reports 1987 and 1988. (CEU/AML Ann Rep), SDD-HBMD internal publications, Edinburgh

Hedges, J 1974-5 'Excavation of two Orcadian burnt mounds at Liddle and Beaquoy', *Proc Soc Antiq Scot*, 106 (1974-5), 39-96

Jakobsen, J 1928-32 *An Etymological Dictionary of the Norn Language in Shetland*, 2 vol

Owen, O 1985 'Excavations and survey work undertaken on a multi-period settlement site at Kebister, Shetland 1985' *Universities of Durham and Newcastle Archaeological Reports for 1985*, 46-52

Owen, O 1985 *An interim report on excavations and survey work undertaken at Kebister, Shetland, 1985*, University of Durham internal publication

Owen, O and Lowe, C 1986 *An interim report on excavations undertaken at Kebister, Shetland 1986*, SDD-HBMD-CEU internal publication

Owen, O 1987 'Interim report on the survey and excavations undertaken at Kebister, Shetland', *CEU/AML Ann Rep 1987*, 28-39

Owen, O and Smith, B 1988 'Kebister, Shetland: An armorial stone and an archdeacon's teind barn?', *Post-Med Arch*, 22, 1-20

Rideout, J in press 'Carn Dubh, Moulin, Perthshire: Survey and Excavation of an Archaeological Landscape' *Proc Soc Antiq Soc* (in press)

Smith, B 1984 'What is a scattald? Rural communities in Shetland 1400-1900', in Crawford, B (ed.) *Essays in Shetland History*, Lerwick, 100-124

Smith, B 1989 'In the tracks of Bishop Andrew Pictoris of Orkney and Henry Phankouth, Archdeacon of Shetland', *Innes Review*, XL, No. 2, 91-105

Unpublished Sources

Nelson, G *MS Notes*, c1955, Shetland Archives, Lerwick

SA, *Shetland Archives*

SA, D.6/172 *Papers Concerning Appointment of Ransel Men Mainly in the North Mainland and the North Isles 1808-1840s*

SA, D11/179 Records of Charity Meal distributed in 1802

SA, Microfilm, *Tingwall Old Parochial Register, 1709-1855* (=SRO, Tingwall OPR in text)

SRO, *Scottish Record Office*

SRO, GD190/box 33, *Smythe and Methven Papers*

SRO, RH4/102, *Dundas Rental, 1777*

SRO, RH9/15/124, *Resignation of Lands in Orkney and Shetland to the Crown by Sir John Arnot, 1615*

SRO, RH9/15/176, *Copy Zetland Scat Rental, 1716-17*

SRO, RS47/1 *Register of Sasines*

PREHISTORIC SITES IN THE SHETLAND LANDSCAPE

A GIS STUDY OF MAINLAND SHETLAND

Mike Canter

Walk a hundred paces from almost any road in Shetland and you will be looking at a landscape that has not altered very much over the past 2000 years. Geology and climate have limited the effects of many modern agricultural practices. This may not be a good thing for those living on the land, but for the landscape or archaeology enthusiast it is a blessing that should not be ignored.

Amongst the interesting humps and bumps are Neolithic oval houses and mounds of burnt stones from the Bronze Age. Some areas have many such sites, whilst others are completely empty. Why? What features made a family choose that location for their house? Perhaps there were no reasons and the locations are purely random. If so, forget analysis and enjoy the walk.

The location of oval houses found on Mainland, Shetland, and adjacent islands, is shown in fig 15. Some very large areas show a complete absence of sites, and where oval houses do occur they appear to form clusters. The location map of burnt mound sites, fig 16, also shows this phenomenon. Why were some areas strongly favoured for such prehistoric sites, whilst others were apparently disliked?

In an attempt to find answers, the locations of 380 prehistoric sites were analysed with respect to a number of geographical factors such as geology, height above sea level, climate and degree of hill slope. The analysis was conducted within a Geographical Information System (GIS). For the reader interested in technicalities, the method used and data sources are given at the end of the paper.

Oval Houses

Fig 15 shows the distribution of the 158 Neolithic oval house locations studied. They appear as about six clusters plus a few isolated examples. There are no doubt others lurking in the records and on the hills, indeed several of those in Dunrossness, Whalsay and Mavis Grind are shown in the records as Neolithic round houses, but having "oval" dimensions.

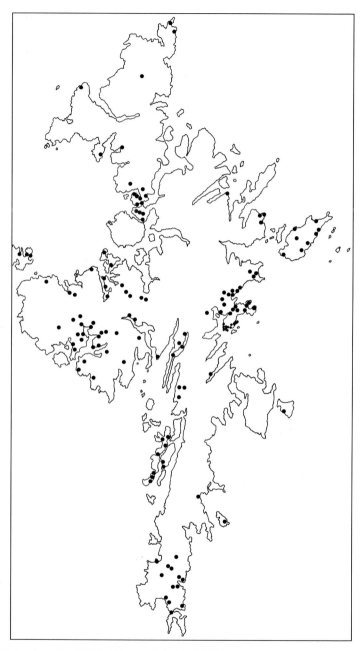

Fig 15. Locations of Neolithic Oval Houses, Shetland Mainland.

48

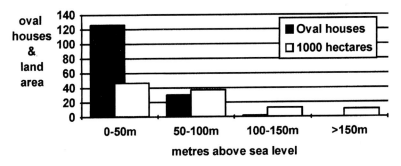

Fig15.1. Oval houses v Height above sea level.

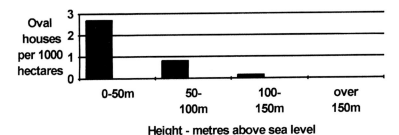

Height - metres above sea level

Fig 15.2. Oval house density v Height above sea level.

Fig 15.1 shows the number of houses and the area of land within each elevation band. Figure 15.2 shows these two components resolved into house density per 1000 hectares. This latter statistic has been taken in this paper as an indicator of preference, i.e. oval houses were preferentially built on land below 50m elevation. Fig 16 shows the land below 50 metres elevation. Not only are 126 of the 158 oval houses to be found on such land, but it can be seen that many of the remainder are adjacent to it.

A similar preference is shown for land within 0.5 km of the sea. Changes in sea level and coastline mean that neither the 0.5 km or the 50 metres elevation statements should taken as an exact measure of the preferred region. They do however appear to be a sound starting point when looking for the Neolithic in today's landscape. Both of these may reflect the same thing, a desire to be housed within easy reach of the sea.

Fig 16. Oval houses — land below 50 metres elevation.

Whilst the above map provides an indication of one major geographical influence on oval house siting , it is not the whole story. Other factors seem to have influenced just where, within the above areas, the houses were built.

The hillslopes on which the houses are situated were examined in terms of both the severity of the slope and its aspect, i.e. the direction it faced. 97% of the houses are on land with a slope between zero and 13°. Over this range there was little variation in house density.

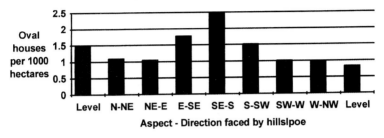

Fig 17. Oval houses v Aspect.

On the other hand the aspect of the slope does appear to have played a part in house site selection. Fig 17 indicates a preference for a SE to S aspect followed by E to SE. The east to south facing quadrant holds 37.3% of the oval houses.

Geology, or more probably the surface effects of the underlying geology, seem to have been one of the deciding factors. Shetland's geology is complex and therefore in this initial study use has been made of the simplified classification entitled "Geological sketch-map of Shetland" in (Mykura,1976).

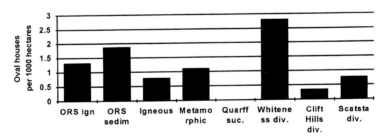

Fig 18. Oval houses v Geology.

The area of the Whiteness Division geology is clearly shown as the most densely populated in fig.18, This is followed by areas of Sedimentary Old Red sandstone. These two geological categories cover only 40% of the area but contain 62% of the oval houses. The map in fig 19 shows the land that has the above geology, and is below 50m in elevation, i.e. where both criteria are met. Apart from the group of houses near Mavis Grind, other types of geology seem to have been avoided. This cluster seems to elude any criteria other than the 50m elevation.

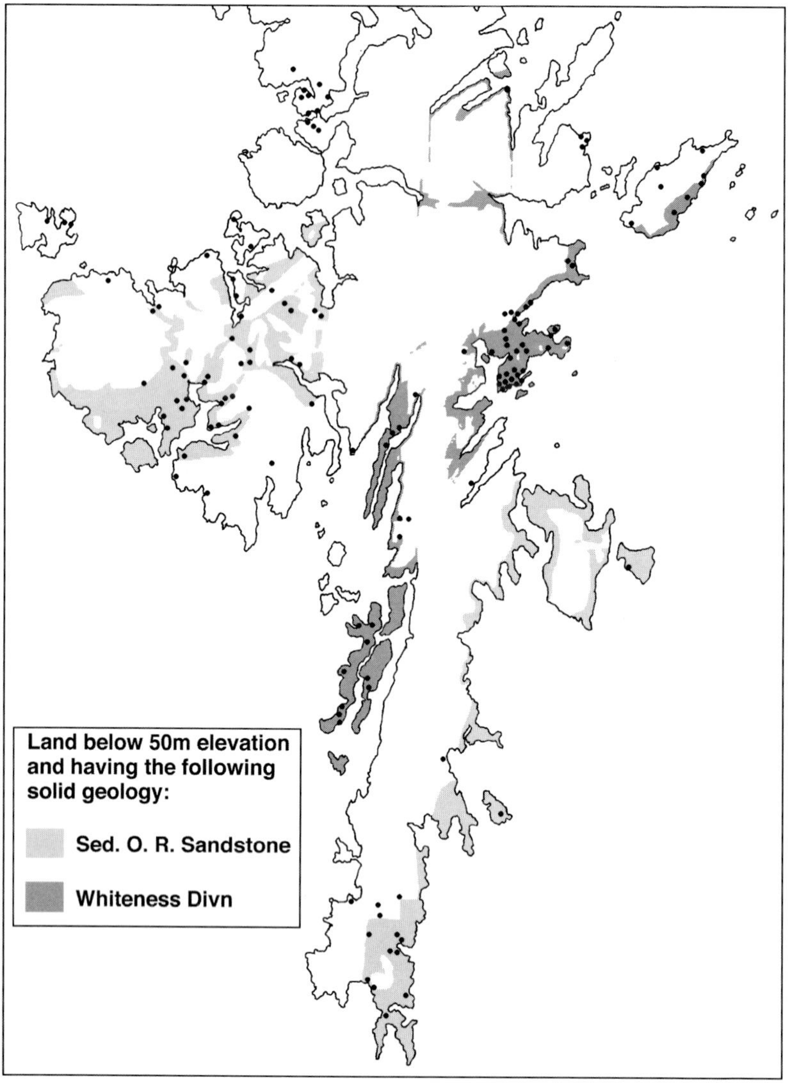
Land below 50m elevation and having the following solid geology:
Sed. O. R. Sandstone
Whiteness Divn

Fig 19. Oval houses — Preferred geology and elevation.

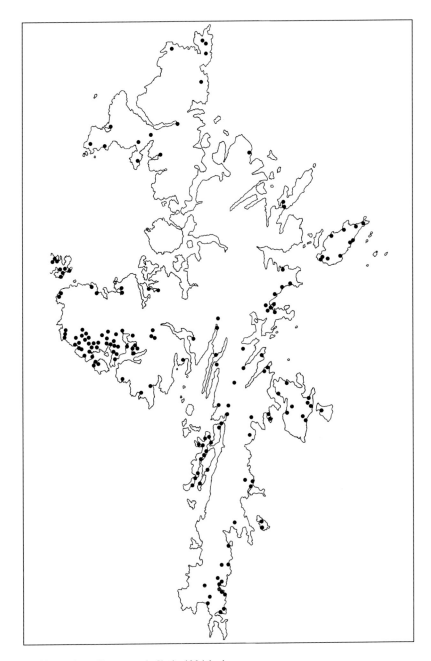

Fig 20. Locations of burnt mounds, Shetland Mainland.

Burnt Mounds

Shetland is rich in the archaeological monuments known as burnt mounds. The mounds were not burnt, but the stones that make up the mound were heated by fire. Having been used to heat up something (probably water) the stones were then cast into heaps. These heaps of scorched stone are usually found today as grass covered mounds. The locations of the 222 burnt mounds analysed in this exercise were taken from Buckley (1990) and are shown in fig 20.

Burnt mounds showed an even stronger affinity for land below 50m than did oval houses. 198 of the 222 being found in such a position. None were found to be above 100 metres elevation

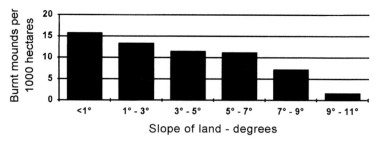

Fig 21. Burnt mound density and slope of land.

As can be seen from fig 21 the slope of land seems to have had some influence on the location of burnt mounds, the site density diminishing as the slope of the land increases.

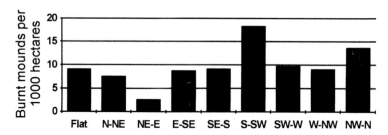

Fig 22. Burnt mounds and aspect.

The direction faced by the hillside may have played a part in positioning the activity from which the mounds arise. Fig 22 shows the greatest density to occur on S-SW facing slopes, but there is also a somewhat smaller peak for slopes with a NW-N aspect. Facing S-SW would have given greatest exposure to the prevailing winds, and may therefore have created hotter fires. Why NW-N? well what aspect would you choose to watch the Simmer Dim whilst having an evening feast?

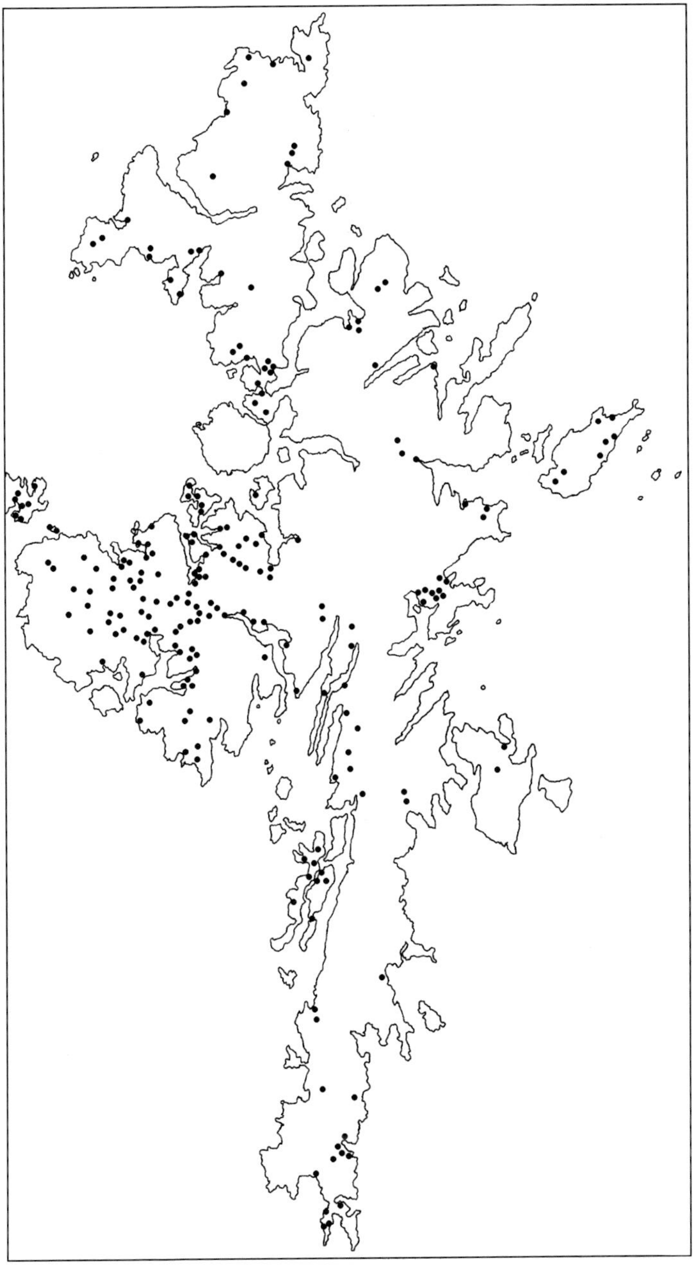

Fig 23. Locations of cairns, Shetland Mainland.

Cairns

Another significant group of prehistoric sites are the many cairns which are to be found upon Shetlands' uplands. Fig 23 shows the location of more than 200 cairns, and indicates that many are found in similar areas to the oval houses and burnt mounds already considered. Indeed they all seem to share many of the same geographical preferences. Cairns are often considered to be hill-top features, and indeed some are. Of the 226 examined 70% were located on the 44% of the land that is below the 50 m level, hardly a bias in favour of high ground.

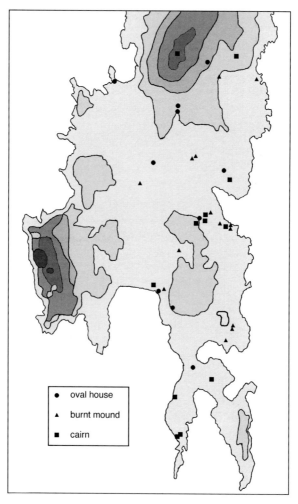

Fig 24. Prehistoric sites found in Dunrossness.

Neolithic, Bronze Age, or just Prehistoric?

Stepping back from the detail to take a general look at the areas in which these archaeological sites occur, it becomes apparent that burnt mounds are found in the same areas in which oval houses occur. Many of the cairns also appear in the same areas. The intimacy of the site mix shown in areas such as Dunrossness, fig 24, makes them look like different functions of the same communities. A similar mix of such sites may be found in many parts of Shetland.

Oval houses are regarded as Neolithic however, whereas burnt mounds are regarded as typical Bronze Age features. Did people of different periods and cultures choose to occupy the same relatively small areas of Mainland Shetland? If so, why? The quantities of fuel and stone implied by the numerous burnt mounds suggests that a large number of people were at work. Where did they live? Is it reasonable to suppose that people who mastered hot stone technology, did not have stone building technology? If they did build in stone, why are there few remains of houses labelled "Bronze Age" when those of the earlier period are so plentiful? It seems probable that burnt mounds and at least some oval houses may have co-existed.

The vertical distribution of the three types of archaeological site are considered together in fig 25. This shows the percentage of each site type found at various elevations. Burnt mounds tend to be nearer sea level than oval houses, with cairns tending to occur at higher elevations. So if you find an oval house, look uphill for the cairns and downhill for the burnt mounds.

The sites were also examined on the basis of the agricultural capability of the land on which the sites stand. The scale used by the Macaulay Institute was simplified to the three categories in fig 26 to show general trends rather than complex detail.

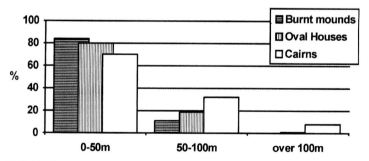

Fig 25. Height above sea level.

Gathering stone is easier on stony ground, so it is probably not surprising to find that the majority of cairns, other than clearance cairns, are on poor agricultural land. The use of large boulders for the base course of oval houses may be the reason for the high number of houses on poor land. On the other hand more burnt mounds are located on good land than poor. This may indicate a connection with agricultural activities or produce. Could the hot stones have been the corn drying kilns of prehistoric Shetland?

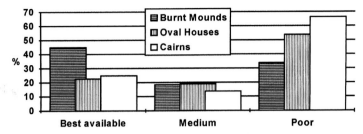

Fig 26. Land capability for agriculture.

Peat, Sand and Other Problems

Fig 27 shows the areas of blanket peat in central Mainland Shetland. Clearly the oval houses and burnt mounds are found in the areas that are not, at the present time, covered by such peat.

Why have so few sites been found in peat covered areas?
Were the areas avoided by prehistoric people
* because the peat was already there?
* or because they were exposed and wet, although not yet peat covered?
* or are the sites there but not yet found?
* because they are covered by peat and can't be found?
* or because the terrain is so difficult the archaeologists have not thoroughly explored them?

Wind blown sand may be hiding archaeological sites in areas such as the south of Dunrossness, (Lamb 1985) and many others will no doubt be submerged by the rise in sea level since the prehistoric period, whilst those patches of Shetland that lend themselves to good agriculture may have already eradicated the sites that they once held. There are nevertheless large areas on which prehistoric features remain to be discovered.

Good walking , but please shut the gate!

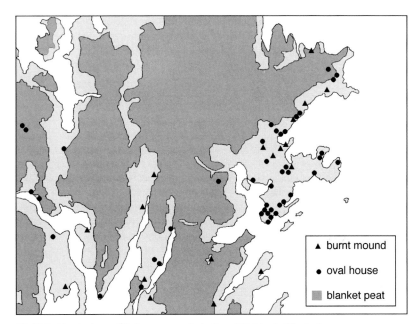

Fig 27. Prehistoric sites and blanket peat cover in the Central Mainland of Shetland.

GIS and the Method of Analysis

The above analyses were undertaken within a geographical information system, (GIS), (Burrough P.A. 1986) A number of computer based maps were created each on a different geographical theme, such as solid geology, elevation, or the degree of hill slope. The locations of the prehistoric sites were culled from the literature or extracted from the Shetland Sites & Monuments Record, (Turner V.E. 1994) and transferred into a somewhat smaller relational database alongside the GIS.

Archaeological sites of the required type, for instance oval houses, were then selected and their locations translated into a file of eastings and northings. The site locations were cross tabulated with the classifications on each thematic map. This provided a listing of the number of sites on each class of land. It also calculated the area of each class of land, permitting the relative site densities to be assessed.

Thematic Maps

The following themes have been mapped, and used in this study.

1.   Land elevation in 50m bands, Based upon O.S. 1:63360, 1934
2.   Distance from sea in 0.5 km bands, Calculated within the GIS.

3. Aspect (direction of slope), as eight 45° classes. Calculated from theme 1 above.

4. Hill slope angle as 15 classes, calculated from theme 1 above.

5. Solid Geology, based upon sketch map in Mykura, (1976)

6. Annual Rainfall as three classes Based upon Dry & Robertson, (1982)

7. Climate as four classes. Based upon Dry & Robertson (1982)

8. Areas of blanket peat

This was a computer based study, and one aim was to view the whole area on the screen. The size of Mainland Shetland resulted in a minimum identifiable area, one pixel, of 150m x 150m. Each such area is given a generalised value, be it height, aspect or geological type. The results are therefore a general guide.

Applying GIS to smaller areas of land should give more precise results. Work has already started on this, but the results will still be theoretical. They may be an aid to the interpretation of what is out there on the ground, but they should not be taken as a substitute for walking, looking and getting a feel for the landscape.

References

Buckley V. (Ed.), (1990), Burnt Offerings, Wordwell Ltd. Dublin.

Dry F.T.& Robertson J.S., (1982), Soil and Land capability for Agriculture: Orkney and Shetland, The Macaulay Institute for Soil Research, Aberdeen

Lamb R.G. (1985), Prehistory Under Sand, in Shetland Archaeology, Ed. B.Smith, The Shetland Times Ltd., Lerwick

Mykura W., (1976), Brit. Reg. Geology: Orkney and Shetland, HMSO Edinburgh.

Ordnance Survey, (1932), 1:63360, 3rd Revision, Southampton.

Turner V.E., (1994), Sites and Monuments Record, Shetland Amenity Trust, Lerwick.

BEYOND THE BURNT MOUND:

THE SOUTH NESTING PALAEOLANDSCAPE PROJECT

S. J. Dockrill, J. M. Bond and T. P. O'Connor

Introduction

An intensive programme of archaeological work within the South Nesting landscape was carried out between 1991 and 1994 by the Department of Archaeological Sciences, University of Bradford under the direction of S.J.Dockrill, and Val Turner of the Shetland Amenity Trust. This work was funded by the British Academy, British Petroleum (Sullom Voe), Shetland Amenity Trust, the Society of Antiquaries (London), the Society of Antiquaries of Scotland and the University of Bradford. The authors would also like to acknowledge the help of Rhoda and Alan Sandison, Jennie and Andy Bradley, Carol and Walter Hunter and the people of South Nesting. The South Nesting Project's research theme was the study of a class of monument known as the burnt mound and its location within its contemporary landscape. This was achieved by integrating intensive archaeological survey, environmental sampling and targeted excavation.

The Problem of Burnt Mounds

Burnt mounds form a class of monument common in both Shetland and Orkney, but have a wider distribution throughout Scotland (Ferguson 1990, 178-192) and beyond. Both burnt mounds and the hot stone technology which they represent, have been the subject of fierce archaeological debate resulting in two international conferences (Buckley 1990, Hodder and Barfield 1991). Burnt mounds (normally of a crescent or horseshoe shape) are formed from the discard of fire-shattered stones and are associated with a water tank (in many instances stone lined).

Several alternative theories have been used to explain these monuments; the first is that they are associated with cooking (Hedges 1977, 74-5 and Barber 1990, 96), the second that they are associated with sweat baths or saunas (Barfield and Hodder, 1987, 370-379 and Barfield 1991, 59-67). A third theory explaining the features associated with burnt mounds suggests that some of these sites may be associated with fulling and dyeing of woollen textiles (Jeffery 1991, 97).

The first systematic excavation of a burnt mound complex in the Northern Isles took place in the 1970s. Two sites, Liddle and Beaquoy, were excavated by John Hedges in Orkney, and both sites revealed the presence of structures. Hedges described these buildings as being permanent structures which looked like domestic houses (Hedges 1977, 82). He also noted that the distribution of burnt mounds coincided with the "best agricultural land" (*ibid*.). This view of Liddle as representing a domestic settlement was maintained by Barber in his review of the Scottish evidence (Barber 1990b, 98). Are, however, the structures such as Liddle *really* domestic, or do they represent a more specialised function which is associated with the use of the burnt mound?

A major flaw in the argument that many burnt mounds represent settlement sites in the Northern Isles is that of the position of the site at the local level. The location of burnt mounds examined on a large scale may coincide with good land but the positioning of these sites at the local scale suggests that many of them occur at places which would have been unfavourable for domestic occupation. Liddle, for example at the "global" scale is associated with relatively fertile land. At a local scale, however, the monument is adjacent to this land but is actually in a wet boggy area, with environmental data indicating that these conditions were also prevalent when the burnt mound was in use. Hedges himself discusses the association of burnt mounds with a "a non-saline water source — be it a spring, river, or just boggy ground" (Hedges 1977, 61-63).

Other factors, such as the morphology (form) of the structures at burnt mounds and also the artefact assemblage, do not support a domestic "settlement" context. The form of the building shares a similarity of building style with other prehistoric structures (for example Liddle and a house structure from the Ness of Gruting are comparable in terms of size and ground plan structures (Øvrevik 1990, 147)), but the furbishments are dissimilar, with the centre of the Liddle structure being dominated by the water tank rather than the hearth. Hedges describes the artefact assemblage of burnt mounds as being "few and, by and large , unimpressive" (1977, 67). The excavations at Liddle and Beaquoy produced flint, pottery and coarse stone artefacts including hammer stones, quern stones, pot lids, perforated stones and ard shares (*ibid*.). Such finds may not be in a true "domestic context"; they may have entered the archaeological record either by being discarded at the site or by being reused, whether as building materials or as stone for heating.

To summarise, it would appear that burnt mounds fulfil a specialised function (whatever that may be) within a settled landscape with their position and construction being determined to fulfil that role: form and location are determined by function.

If these "Liddle type" structures associated with burnt mounds are not domestic houses, then where and how were the users of these burnt mounds living?

The South Nesting Palaeolandscape Project was conceived with this research question in mind. The project was planned as an archaeological study of the South Nesting landscape bringing together a programme of intensive fieldwalking, electronic mapping, detailed recording of monuments, environmental sampling and targeted exploratory excavation. In order to study the prehistoric landscape, and to isolate features which might be contemporary with the burnt mounds, it was decided to survey all traces of human impact on the landscape, including features which were clearly the product of the more recent "crofting" landscape.

The South Nesting landscape was selected for study because it contained a known concentration of burnt mounds (Calder 1965, 81; Shetland Sites and Monuments Record) situated within a fertile belt of Girlsta Limestone rock. This coincides with the later settlement concentration formed by the townships of Skellister, Garth and Vassa. Both the modern and the past settlement patterns within South Nesting appear to have been shaped by the geology of this area. The Girlsta Limestone rocks are predominantly calcite marble. The area immediately to the north is formed of psammites with gneissic permeation belonging to the Colla Firth Group (Mykura, 1976). Much of this area is today covered by blanket peat. To the south of the Girlsta Limestone, psammites of the Wadbister Ness Group form irregular hills used today as hill pasture, with another Girlsta Limestone outcrop forming the peninsula of Gletness (*ibid.*). The survey area provided large samples of both the Girlsta Limestone belt and the hills to the south and the Gletness peninsula. The area to the north was not surveyed due to the overburden of blanket peat which obscured the visibility of earlier landscape features.

The South Nesting Burnt Mound Investigations

The emphasis of research into burnt mounds within the Project centred on two monuments. The first was an eroding burnt mound complex at Trowie Loch (HU4723 5381 & HU4725 5380), which was excavated in order to provide environmental samples from stratified contexts, and stratified artefacts which could be compared with those from other sites. The excavation would also provide important information relating to the location of the burnt mound and its use over time. A second burnt mound at Benston (Survey Site 177, HU4634 5419) provided further evidence concerning the siting of burnt mounds together with a vegetational history which could be linked archaeologically to the burnt mound.

The Trowie Loch Burnt Mounds, Vadill of Garth

This burnt mound complex was first described by Calder in his major work on the monuments of Shetland (Calder 1965, 80). Calder listed the site as "Vadill of Garth", after the inlet on which it lay. Later works, including the Shetland Sites and Monuments Record and the gazetteer of burnt mounds in Buckley (1990), list the site as "Trowie Loch". To minimise confusion, the more recent name will be used.

Calder recorded the site as a single burnt mound of about 90ft in diameter, interpreting the channel through the middle as the result of tidal action and erosion cutting it into two (a landward mound, Mound A, Survey Site 251 and a larger mound which is, in effect, a small inter tidal island Mound B, Survey Site 252). At the highest spring tides, Mound A is also almost cut off from the mainland. The channel between the two mounds virtually disappears at the lowest tidal ebb,

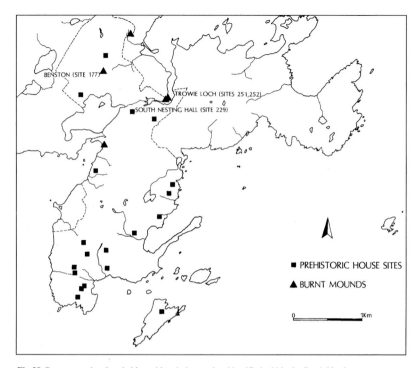

Fig 28. Burnt mound and probable prehistoric house sites identified within the South Nesting survey area.

revealing burnt and shattered stones which eroded from the two and become mixed with later debris.

The mounds lie at the head of the Vadill of Garth where the stream running from Trowie Loch meets the tidal waters of the Voe (fig 28). The water around the mounds is saline; bladderwrack (*Fucus vesiculosus*) grows in abundance around the site. The tidal changes affect the mounds drastically, the spring tides rising halfway up the side of the larger mound (B). These tides have been a serious cause of erosion to the sites, eating away at the margins of both areas and creating small erosion platforms.

The sites at Trowie Loch are scheduled but eroding badly, and so needed a course of action which minimised further damage, whilst allowing the maximum amount of information to be gained from the damaged monuments without hastening the effects of erosion. Before excavation began, a detailed survey of the mounds was also undertaken, using both conventional and geophysical techniques.

The excavation, directed by Julie Bond, was limited to the clearing of the beach deposits and investigation of underlying material, and the cleaning-back and recording of eroded sections. This activity formed two areas of excavation, Area A on the smaller landward mound, and Area B, the excavated area of the larger off-

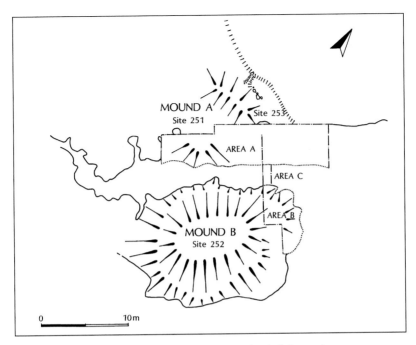

Fig 29. The Trowie Loch burnt mound complex showing the archaeological excavation areas.

shore Mound B (fig 29). A trench connecting these two trenches, Area C, allowed the deposits under the tidal channel to be investigated.

The Shore Burnt Mound (Mound A)

When the beach deposits were cleared in the intertidal area on the landward mound (fig 30) it was immediately apparent that the site was not a single burnt mound cut by an erosion channel, but two separate mounds. There was a hearth well below the tide line which had been protected in part from erosion by the compaction of the deposit and the covering sand. Subsequent excavation showed that there was a rubble-filled pit to the north of the hearth, slightly higher up the beach, lying between the two "arms" of Mound A and partially buried by slumped rubble from the western arm. The western arm of the mound had largely resisted erosion, but the rest of the exposed area has been eroded down to a tidal platform, covered with sand, small pebbles and some modern debris. The area later found to contain the pit was, on first examination, still covered by a small area of crumbling peat and turf.

The earliest excavated strata were found beneath the "beach" deposit of sand and pebbles at the edge of the channel. South of the pit were two narrow bands of

65

Fig 30. Excavation of the shore burnt mound (A).

humic peaty material interleaved with a sandy pebbly layer which became progressively thinner as they rose up the beach, suggesting that the mound was situated on or near the lip of the peat basin. These humic layers could be traced back and equated with the submerged peat recorded between the two mounds (Area C, see below). The narrow peaty bands were sealed by the upcast from the pit, suggesting that in contrast to the Inter-Tidal Burnt Mound (B, below), the Shore Burnt Mound (A) developed on the edge of the peat basin.

The first sign of human activity on the site was a burnt stone spread lying beneath the remains of a hearth-like feature. Excavation of the hearth revealed a spread of burnt material forming an open hearth or fire floor with at least two separate phases of use. In turn the hearth itself was sealed by the upcast from the pit and by slumped rubble from the westerly arm of the mound, suggesting that the hearth may have been associated with a different tank in an unexcavated area, and that when the excavated pit was open, this hearth had fallen out of use. Alternatively the upcast from the pit may represent a recut or a cleaning-out of an older pit feature contemporary with the hearth discussed above. Whichever hypothesis is favoured, at least three separate phases of burnt mound usage are represented.

The pit itself lies between the two crescent arms of the mound, the whole facing SSE. On excavation it was found to be full of burnt rubble and partially covered by mound slump, and a thin peat had developed over its surface, presumably because of the restricted drainage conditions beneath. The pit was surrounded by a hard-packed halo of the same silty clay material which formed its sides, at present interpreted as upcast from the cutting or later emptying, although it may possibly be a deliberately-added lining of waterproof material; the archaeological cleaning of the sides of the pit seemed to increase the flow of groundwater into it. Two layers of slumped silty material beneath the rubble fill at the base of the pit suggest that the feature had remained open for some time.

Investigation of the central depression in the mound revealed an area of flagging, bordered by two orthostats, which appeared to be part of a substantial structure. Excavation of the mound material to the west exposed a further stone alignment which may well be part of the same structure.

The mound was subsequently covered with a thin layer of blanket peat, which was succeeded in the east part of the site by a thick lynchet of agricultural soil, presumably a field boundary, resembling the material found in the cleaned cliff section to the east.

The final phase of the site, probably post-Medieval in date, was the use of the lynchet and the easternmost slope of the burnt mound as the setting for a boat noost (site 253). A bank was constructed at the northern end of this hollow and an iron stake inserted as a tying-up point. Iron boat-nails and a fragment of copper-alloy foil, found on the beach below the noost, testify to its use.

Inter-tidal Burnt Mound (Area B)

The larger mound, situated in the inter-tidal zone (B), was beginning to be substantially eroded, both by the action of the tides and by the rabbits which have burrowed into and through the top of the mound. The apex of the mound is known locally to have been used as a kelp-burning area at one time. The erosion damage was mostly confined to the easternmost edge of the mound and to the northern edge which faces the tidal channel, where undercutting was pronounced. To the east, erosion has produced a tidal platform of burnt stone from which the upper layers of the mound have been stripped, at the base of a "cliff-face" of eroding mound. To the south of this face, on the edge of the mound, substantial orthostats which may be structural are visible.

Archaeological work on this mound was limited to section recording, and the partial excavation of the tidal platform (fig 31). The core of the mound consisted of deposits of red and black ash; soil samples were taken to ascertain the nature of the fuel, but preliminary examination suggested peat or a similar material. This core of ash layers is sealed by a succession of further stone and ash tips, in turn sealed by a peaty, ashy soil (perhaps the result of the reported kelp burning) and a loamy topsoil.

Excavation of a sondage (small trench) along the north-facing section (made more difficult by the water level in the channel, which necessitated continual pumping) showed that the waste tips of burnt stone were sitting on submerged peat at this edge of the mound.

Fig 31. Excavation of the off-shore burnt mound (B).

Between the Mounds (Area C)

In order to discover the relationship between what were now recognised as two burnt mounds in close proximity, a slit trench was excavated in the channel between the mounds in between tides (fig 29). This trench showed, beneath a shallow covering of sand and pebbles, a depth of up to 0.7m of peat, overlying a blue-grey silt also containing plant remains (fig 32). This peat could be traced as it rose upwards onto the "beach" of the shore mound (A). These earlier layers of beach material are overlain by the upcast from the Area A pit, securely placing them in the site stratigraphy.

The relationship of the peat with the inter-tidal mound (Mound B) is more problematic, and means that the relationship between the two mounds is still unsettled. The northernmost mound material from Mound B can be traced in the trench C section where it rests directly on the peat with no intervening sand or silt; the peat appears to be abruptly truncated where it meets the burnt stone. Slumping of the mound material suggests this may be an erosion feature; a southern edge of the trench which extended into the inter-tidal mound (B), under the deepest part of the mound, the mound material and ash was seen to sit on a silty grey-black layer, which in turn sealed the sedge peat described above. The mineral soil appears to be a buried soil equivalent to that found in corings in the Vadill, where it also overlay sedge peat. This may have been an immature soil which was beginning to form on the surface of an old basin peat. Towards the channel between the mounds, this silty soil becomes more diffuse and disturbed, and is covered with more peat. Under the centre of the mound it is sealed by a 10cm depth of black soil, not present elsewhere in the section, sealed in turn by the ash and stone of the mound.

Fig 32. The trench between the mounds (excavation area C).

The British Regional Geology volume for Orkney and Shetland (Mykura 1976, 110-111) notes that submerged peat is common in the sheltered voes and sounds of Shetland, citing this as part of the evidence for the continuous submergence of Shetland since the last Ice Age. In this respect, Vadill of Garth would seem to be typical. Berry and Johnston (1980, 44-5) note that many of these voes are so sheltered that the sea has been unable to substantially erode the peat, and that in many instances on tidal shores "peat can be seen just below a protecting layer of pebbles". Coring and the excavation of small test pits around the shores of the Vadill of Garth showed this to be exactly the case. Regrettably, examination of the peat cores showed very poor preservation of pollen, and so no pollen analysis could thus be undertaken, although examination of surviving macrofossils showed sedges (*Carex* spp.) to be common.

Finds

It had been hoped that the geology of the area might be more favourable to the preservation of bone than the more acid areas of Shetland. In the event this seems not to be the case although over 100 small finds were recorded from the two mounds. In addition to the 6 iron nails and the copper-alloy fragment from the noost area, the finds consisted of pottery shards, coarse stone tools and crudely-struck quartzite with the majority of these finds coming from Area B. When the limited amount of material excavated and the usually sparse nature of finds from burnt mounds is considered, this assemblage represents a useful addition to the database for Bronze Age Shetland.

The pottery assemblage includes a base and several rim shards. The base is flat and shows evidence of being coil-built. The fabric is orange-brown on its outer surface, dark grey on its inner, which also preserves a black organic deposit on the vessel wall. The fabric is steatite-tempered. Three rim fragments in the same fabric show a plain flat rim and undecorated, slightly rounded sides. Some of the other fragments also show sooting.

A Burnt Mound and its Environment Uncovered at Benston

Excavations were undertaken by T.P. O'Connor on the burnt mound at Benston (Site 177, fig 28) in order to investigate the relationship between the mound and adjacent and underlying sediments. The burnt mound, 14m (E-W axis) by 11m, was rather slumped, but still typically horseshoe-shaped, with a distinct hollow on the south-east side. Rabbits had burrowed extensively into the west end of the mound, suggesting that it consisted of softer, more ashy, material there than at the east end which was stonier. A trench, 3m x 1m, was cut into the eastern margin of the mound, positioned so as to cut the edge of the mound, the slumped material which formed a narrow 'apron' around that side, and the adjacent level ground (fig 33).

The modern soil was found to pass from a thin, grey, friable soil on the mound itself to a black humified peat at the east end of the trench, with a continuous gradation between these extremes. At the west end of the trench, the soil overlay *in situ* mound material, a dense mass of burnt and unburnt stone in a fine ashy matrix. To the east, this became a looser rubble, which thinned to become sparse stones in a peaty matrix. At the east end of the trench, modern peat overlay the sparse rubble, which in turn overlay a less humified brown peat. Excavation became problematic at about 55cm below the modern surface, as water began to issue from the sectioned mound material at the west end of the trench. The mound appeared to be supporting a water table somewhat higher than that of the surrounding terrain, producing a spring line within the trench. This had also been noted at Trowie Loch. The north and west sections of the trench showed that the brown peat extended underneath the mound, and thus pre-dated it. The peat was cored at the east end of the trench from immediately beneath the burnt mound material to close to the base of the peat nearly 1m below. This core was subsampled for pollen, and the results of the analysis are outlined below .

In brief, the excavation showed the burnt mound to have been constructed in, and on, a pre-existing mire, probably in an area of wet, sedge-dominated pasture not unlike that surrounding the site today. The apparent 'apron' around the mound appears to be material which has slumped and eroded from the mound, and may represent erosion during the first few months following the last use of the mound prior to the establishment of a turf cover. The eastern end of the mound was of close-packed burnt stone. The examination of a sample of the constituent stones has

Fig 33. Excavation of the burnt mound at Benston.

shown no obvious preference for any particular geological type. Augering at the other end of the mound indicated less stone and more ash, and black ashy material was encountered within the mound 'hollow'. Benston may therefore be quite complex, and perhaps multi-phase in use and construction.

Three cores were taken through the pre-mound peat at Benston, at the eastern end of the excavation trench. Core A and Core B were parallel, and both extended downwards from the point at which the brown peat and the modern peat met. Together with Core C, taken from the base of the excavation downwards, the three cores sampled rather less than a metre of the pre-burnt mound peat. The results of pollen analysis of these cores are reported below.

Auger transects were taken to the south and the east of the mound, in order to establish the extent of the pre-mound peat, and to determine its thickness. Sampling established that the peat extends over a relatively small area and is about 1m thick. Towards the base, the peat contains more mineral particles, in places passing into a dark grey-brown humic silty clay. The peat was traced for at least a further 20m east of the trench, but thinned and quickly disappeared within 12m to the south. On considering the results of further augering and the local topography together, the burnt mound appears to overlie the north-west corner of a peat deposit measuring only 25m north-south by less than 100m east-west.

Pollen analysis was undertaken by Andrew Hoaen as an undergraduate project, under the supervision of T.P.O'Connor, and with the advice and help of Dr Margaret Atherden. The account of the pollen analysis which follows is based on Hoaen's BSc dissertation. The pollen record at the site was divided into two zones. The differences between the zones lies in the relative abundance of pollen in major plant groups (taxa). The zones are described in detail in the accompanying table. The lowest 25cm of the core contained a high proportion of sedge pollen, with high counts of ling pollen and spores from sphagnum moss. Although tree pollen was scarce, counts for birch, pine and hazel were higher in this zone than further up the sequence. Pollen from the herbaceous plants were mostly from relatively tall-growing taxa such as meadowsweet and the umbellifers. The succeeding 36cm was also dominated by sedge pollen, but with higher proportions of grass pollen, and less tree pollen, fern spores and sphagnum spores. Large grass pollen grains, attributable to cereal grasses, first appear in the sequence in this zone. This upper zone has been tentatively divided, on the basis of small changes in the herbaceous taxa represented. In the topmost 6cm of the peat cores, birch pollen shows a slight increase, and pollen of sea plantain, meadowsweet, and docks increase, as do fern spores. Cereal pollen declines in this zone.

Table 1

Zonation Recognised in the Pollen Data From Benston

SN177/1 Calluna-Sphagnum-Cyperaceae zone (133-108cm).
This zone is characterised by high values of Cyperaceae, over 40% of total, and high values of *Calluna* pollen and *Sphagnum* spores. These taxa maintain levels above 20% throughout the zone. This zone contains the highest levels of arboreal pollen, in particular *Betula*, *Pinus*, and *Corylus*, all with levels over 2%, and with a *Betula* maximum of 5%. Tall herbs such as *Filipendula*, *Succissa* type and Umbelliferae type all attain their maximum frequency in this zone, and ferns and mosses are also well represented. Grass pollen(=Poaceae) values are quite low in comparison with later zones, and other herbs such as Caryophyllaceae undiff. and Chenopodiaceae are at their lowest level in the diagram.

SN177/2 Cyperaceae-Gramineae zone (106-70cm).
This zone is characterised by very high levels of Cyperaceae, generally over 60% of all pollen, occasionally rising as high as 70% of pollen sum. Levels of grass pollen increase at the base of this zone to a maximum of 31% at 106cm and remain above 15% throughout the zone. During this zone there is the first appearance of cereal pollen at 94cm.

Within zone SN177/2, Compositae liguliflorae undiff. reaches a maximum of 7% at 106cm and remains at relatively high levels until 82cm. *Ranunculus acris* type and Ranunculaceae undiff. are also well represented in the diagram. Levels and occurrence of Caryophyllaceae undiff. are higher than the preceding zone. The increase in Gramineae and Cyperaceae pollen is coupled with a decline in *Sphagnum* spores and in tree pollen. The previously high levels of spores decline, and *Sphagnum* undergoes a marked decline above 104cm to under 2% and remains below this level throughout the rest of the diagram. Overall, the levels and frequency of bracken and fern spores are greatly reduced. *Calluna* values decline but remain constant at about 5% of total pollen for this zone. There is a decline in other Ericales at the same time as for *Calluna*. Values and frequency of occurrence of tall herbs decline through this zone.

Zone SN177/2 has been subdivided into two sub-zones. Briefly, these are distinguished by small changes in the herbaceous component of the diagram. Sub-zone SN177/2a (106-78cm) shows an increase in Compositae liguliflorae type to a maximum of 7% at 106cm and an increased frequency of occurrence of Caryophyllaceae undiff. and Chenopodiaceae. *Ranunculus acris* type becomes continuous after 102cm, and at 94cm there is the first appearance of cereal pollen. Sub-zone SN177/2b (76-70cm) is characterised by an increase in Caryophyllaceae undiff. type associated with an increase in the level of *Betula*, Chenopodiaceae, *Plantago maritima*, *Filipendula*, and Ranunculaceae undiff. pollen, and Filicales spores. There is a drop in the number and frequency of cereal, Compositae liguliflorae type and *Ranunculus acris* type pollen.

The pollen data indicates a vegetational history of general simplicity but subtle in detail. First, the nature of the peat and the high levels of sedge (Cyperaceae) pollen throughout the core indicates that the peat formed in a small mire occupying a limited hollow in the undulating landscape: small sedge-dominated mires are common throughout South Nesting today. The great majority of the pollen and spores probably derive from vegetation growing on the mire surface, with little long-range transport, so the data probably reflect quite local vegetational communities. Second, there is the question of date. The top of the sequence is sealed, but apparently not truncated, by burnt mound material belonging to a monument type perhaps most typical of the early first millennium bc, but extending both earlier and later than this period. The top of the sequence could be loosely assigned to the period 3500-2500 years ago, pending absolute dating. The lowest samples in the core lack any indicators of an early Flandrian date: the presence throughout the core of ribwort plantain (*Plantago lanceolata*) pollen suggests a date later than 4650 bp by analogy with Johansen's results from Murraster (Johansen 1978). The core therefore appears to represents one or two millennia of vegetational development prior to construction of the mound.

There is evidence of prehistoric occupation around the margins of the hollow in which Benston burnt mound is located. 300m to the north-east, at Whalsay Willie's Knowe (Site No 112) there is a prehistoric enclosure with possible house structures on a low knoll. Excavation has yielded evidence of ard-cultivation underneath field dykes associated with the site. Further to the west, similar structures occupy a low hill at Holm of Benston, and fieldwork during 1991-3 has revealed quite a dense pattern of prehistoric settlement across the South Nesting area. It is likely that there was human settlement within a few kilometres of the site throughout the period represented by this pollen diagram, although the immediate area around Benston burnt mound does not appear to have been cultivated or heavily grazed. The abrupt change between zones 1 and 2 may well represent the expansion of grazing onto the mire, and cereal pollen begins to appear in the sequence soon after this vegetational change. It is tempting, although insupportable, to link the agricultural activity here with the site at Whalsay Willie's Knowe. The similarity between the plant community indicated by the pollen from zone 2 and communities to be found on grazed sedge+grass pastures in the area today is surely not coincidental. What is important is the change immediately prior to the construction of the burnt mound. Although interpretation is not obvious, the rise in meadowsweet (*Filipendula*) and reduction in dandelions (Compositae liguliflorae) could indicate a lessening of grazing pressure. The burnt mound appears to have been constructed upon a rather wet area of pasture or former pasture, and thus on land of little value for cultivation.

Close to the northern limit of the project's study area, Edwards *et al,* (1993) have cored at Grunna Water. The topographical location is not dissimilar, although the hollow at Grunna Water contains a shallow loch. More to the point, Edwards et al found that the top 130cm of the Grunna Water peat (Zone GWP6), is dominated by heather (*Calluna*), sphagnum (*Sphagnum*), sedge (Cyperaceae), and some birch (*Betula*). Although the proportions differ from those seen at Benston, a similar vegetation community is indicated. There is finely-divided charcoal in GWP6: a prehistoric house site is located 150m north of the sampling point, on the edge of the topog.ραphical basin. Unlike Benston, however, the Grunna Water mound appears to have been constructed in an area of heather-dominated blanket peat, rather than in a sedge-dominated hollow.

To conclude, the area around Benston was altered by prehistoric activity, probably grazing, as small-scale changes in land-use and intensity of use may have produced a mosaic of plant communities. The use of small mires associated with sites and monuments in an area like South Nesting offer the opportunity to tie in small vegetational changes with evidence of human activity, both local to the site and across the region as a whole.

Burnt Mounds and the Field Survey

The archaeological survey revealed one other previously unrecorded burnt mound, located on a rocky outcrop on the shore of Vassa Voe (HU4631 5312). This burnt mound has been badly eroded by wave action, and is 8 by 1.5m with the long axis oriented N-S. The site has had a concrete post set into it. The exposed coastal section did not show any evidence of fossil soils surviving underneath the mound material.

The addition of only one burnt mound to the archaeological record is not surprising. Burnt mounds by their nature are visible and likely to be recorded, whereas the evidence of their contemporary landscape may be less obvious and so is less likely to have entered the known archaeological record.

The Landscape Beyond the Burnt Mounds

A number of prehistoric house sites within the survey area had been identified and described by Charles Calder. These included the sites discussed above on the Ward of Benston (Calder 1958, 368) and Whalsay Willie's Knowe (Calder 1968, 75-6). The aim of the survey was to identify further evidence of prehistoric settlement together with any surviving evidence of an infrastructure of boundaries and field systems.

The Survey Area contained three zones: land used as outfield grazing during the crofting period within the central belt delineated by the Girlsta Limestone; areas subjected to arable cultivation during the crofting period within the central belt and beyond (eg: Gletness, on a limestone outcrop) and the hill pasture of the Roonies, south of this central belt. In general prehistoric boundaries and evidence of settlement were more complete the less intensively the land had been used since. The remains of the prehistoric field systems within the infield areas was very fragmented with small lengths of boundary survived around the edges of later

Fig 34. Prehistoric field boundary.

crofting fields (fig 34). Although the boundaries were fragmented they do confirm the presence of earlier field systems in this fertile belt.

"House sites" with clearly defined field systems and boundary dykes were identified within the hills to the south. The project would like to thank and acknowledge the help of Robert Leask in the study of this area. One particular complex combining a "house" structure and associated "infield" system is worthy of detailed discussion here. This site is situated on the lower south eastern slope of the Hill of Taing. The "house" is sub-circular with an external diameter of some 13m, the internal space measuring 5 by 7m (fig 35). The surrounding infield excludes animals from an area some 60 by 30m, with a second field enclosure of approximately the same size surviving to the north west. Targeted trial excavation of the northern edge of the house wall indicated that the internal face was edged with large orthostats, with a core of rubble behind, which had apparently been covered with a turf jacket on the outside. Excavation within the infield and across its western boundary indicated the survival of a fossil soil. This soil showed clear signs of human interference, a visible ash and carbon component suggesting that the fields had been manured. No artefacts which could have given the site a specific date were recovered.

South Nesting Hall: A Relict Bronze Age Landscape

One particular area (fig 36) which displayed the problems of fragmentation and reuse was identified by the survey adjacent to the South Nesting Hall. The area is bounded to the west by a small hill, with outcropping rock surrounded to the south

Fig 35. Excavation of the infield area outside a prehistoric house at the Hill of Taing, Gletness.

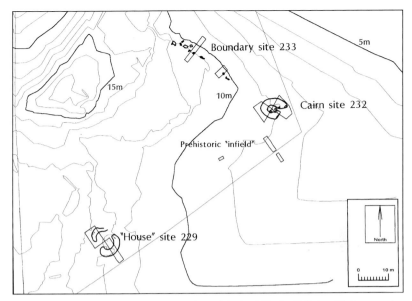

Fig 36. Computer generated plan of the archaeology of the South Nesting Hall site with the excavation trenches shown.

east by a relatively level terrace while to the north east the slope drops sharply to the basin between the Loch of Benston and Trowie Loch. The hill was bounded to the south and east by a hill dyke which encloses traces of a prehistoric landscape. A boundary/lynchet (site 233) and an irregular mound (site 232) formed the northern boundary of the landscape. The large stones which protruded from the mound suggested a central chamber and a "heel" shaped facade facing south east, although these were too fragmentary to be certain without excavation. Earthworks to the west of the hill dyke suggested an oval house form (site 229). The earthworks were surveyed using both conventional and geophysical means and then partially excavated.

Excavation revealed an oval/sub rectangular "house" 10m (NW-SE) by 6m formed by an irregular double faced wall with a core of brown silty clay loam with carbon flecking. The excavated evidence suggests that first the contemporary topsoil was removed from the centre of what was to become the building. An outcrop at the north west end of the structure gave rise to a change in level, perhaps forming a dais or raised bench. There was clear evidence of stone robbing, shown by earth-filled holes which had once held stones (fig 37). It is likely that this monument had been quarried for stone for the adjacent hill dyke, 3.5m to the south. Despite being badly disturbed by this later activity, the remains of a hearth was found in the centre of the structure, represented by some carbonised material and a scorched surface. A number of coarse stone tools were also found associated with

Fig 37. South Nesting Hall house site, where the wall has been "robbed" of stone.

Fig 38. Outside the house site, a midden had built up which contained pottery.

Fig 39. Burial cairn at South Nesting Hall, under excavation.

the structure. Outside the house, adjacent to the south east wall, 25 sherds of prehistoric pottery were recovered from a midden-like deposit (fig 38).

The cairn-like structure was partially excavated in order to discover what it was, its date and how it related to the boundary and the "house" site. The cairn was found to consist of a central chamber 2m in diameter defined by stone blocks (standing up to 0.7m high) which was surrounded by a cairn of small angular stones which formed a monument some 7m in diameter and probably derived from field clearance (fig 39). The monument showed clear signs of having been disturbed, with several large structural stone blocks being rolled out of their original position. Again it is likely that this disturbance was caused by the robbing of medium sized stones for the construction of the hill dyke 8m to the south east of this monument. The large blocks that were either left *in situ* or had been disturbed were presumably those which were too heavy to remove easily. (Even with levers and ropes, it took five excavators to remove one of these blocks from the excavation area). The smaller clearance stones seem to have been too small for reuse and appeared undisturbed. On either side of the central chamber, fragments of pottery and cremated human bone were found. These were fragmented and their position, sealing the cairn material immediately to the side of the chamber, suggests that the finds had been disturbed and discarded when the stone was removed.

The form (shape and construction) of the structure and the discovery of human cremated remains suggest that the site was a funerary monument. The excavated evidence provides little in the way of detail as to whether the disturbed cremated burial or burials represented original or later use. A heel-shaped facade is normally associated with Neolithic chambered cairns, although the use of this type of monument may have extend into the Bronze Age. There is evidence for other "heel shaped" chambered cairns of a similar size at Islesburgh and Mangaster (Henshall 1963, 405). The facade of this cairn, in common with the majority of Shetland chambered cairns, faces approximately SE (Henshall 1963, 148). There was no identifiable evidence of inhumation, although the soil conditions would not have supported the survival of unburnt bone.

A buried fossil soil abutted both the western exterior of the cairn and the western exterior of the oval structure. In the case of the cairn, this was partly sealed by small stone suggesting field clearance. Where it was not affected by iron panning, the soil was a dark reddish brown silty clay loam with carbon flecking. Excavation in a series of trenches between these two monuments and across the early field boundary indicated that this was the same soil and that it was restricted by the boundary. Evidence of ard cultivation could be clearly identified in a number of places. Excavation under and beyond the later hill dyke showed that this soil and the traces of its associated ard cultivation pre-dated this later land division.

The boundary feature had been constructed using large stones which were positioned at the top of the break of slope between the level cultivated terrace and the steep downward slope to the north east. Smaller stones, from field clearance, were found between these large stones and spread away from the boundary down the slope (fig 38). Several coarse broad bladed stone tools, normally interpreted as mattock or spade like implements, were found in association with the boundary, together with a polished stone axe. Other coarse stone tools, including two broken stone ard points, were found during the excavation of the clearance material surrounding the cairn.

The cultivated soil was sampled using several means of analysis including magnetic susceptibility and soil micromorphology, both of which indicated manuring (Dockrill and Simpson 1994, 92). This would have helped to reduce the effects of podsolization and to replenish nutrients, allowing for high yields of barley to have been maintained. Soil micromorphological work from a fossil soil adjacent to the inner infield boundary of the Hill of Taing house site suggested that here a cultivated soil had been improved using peaty turf, ash and organic materials (probably animal manures).

Two radiocarbon dates for the buried soil, one taken from the lower part of the profile and the other from the upper, suggest the possibility of the intensive cultivation spanning the period from late Neolithic until the Iron Age. (SRR-5254, sample depth 25 to 29cm, measured age (C^{14} years BP± 1σ) 1630 ± 45 BP; SRR-5255, sample depth 39 to 41cm, measured age (C^{14} years BP± 1σ) 3620 ± 55 BP.) The finds from the cairn, the "house" site, and the boundary all suggest a Bronze age date. The pottery assemblage from both the cairn and the "house" indicate that these two sites share the same vessel forms and fabrics as those found at the Trowie Loch burnt mound. Although dating based upon the ceramic evidence does not permit us to say that these sites and the buried soil were in use at exactly the same time, it is possible to say that they are elements which form a contemporary or near-contemporary landscape.

Discussion and Conclusions

This paper has focused on the question of identifying the landscape which may be contemporary with the use of burnt mounds. Two burnt mound sites within the survey area (Trowie Loch and Benston) have provided important environmental evidence relating to their location within the landscape. It has been seen that the overall distribution of burnt mounds is restricted to the fertile central South Nesting belt which contains the foci of modern settlement: Skellister, Garth and Vassa. Although fragmented by later use, elements of earlier landscapes were found to survive here. There is a problem in dating many elements of the earlier landscape and in some cases it may not be possible to identify whether a monument is prehistoric in date or not. Targeted excavation has helped, but without the presence of securely dated objects, diagnostic of a particular period, the problem of dating may remain unresolved.

The relic landscape at South Nesting Hall site contains clear evidence of prehistoric settlement and its associated intensive "infield" agriculture. Although physical evidence of prehistoric "infield" agriculture in Shetland is well established around sites such as the Scord of Brouster, these sites lack evidence of the nature of the land management practised. The South Nesting Hall site has provided data, new to Shetland, about prehistoric cultivation methods and manuring practices. At the time of writing, the data are still being studied, and the study of early agricultural soils will also form an important research theme within the Scatness Broch project, (Turner, this volume).

The data from the South Nesting survey points to a distribution of prehistoric settlement across the central Girlsta Limestone belt, south across the Roonies to the Voe of Gletness, in contrast to the burnt mound distribution which is confined to the central belt. This begs the question of which of these settlement sites are contemporary with the burnt mounds, assuming all the burnt mounds share a similar Bronze Age date?

To address this question fully would require the excavation and comparison of all settlement sites. As this is not practical, we are left with the results of the survey and targeted excavation to suggest a possible model which might explain the results. One possible model is that the burnt mound distribution at South Nesting represents a contraction of settlement in the later Bronze Age to the central belt. The more marginal location of the southerly settlements, perhaps established in the later Neolithic and Early Bronze Age, might have become less viable in the deteriorating climatic conditions believed to have occurred in the Later Bronze Age. How the same land was used during the nineteenth and twentieth centuries will be discussed by Robert Leask, Andy Bradley and Jennie Bradley (this volume).

References

Barfield, L.H. and Hodder M.A. 1987, "Burnt mounds as saunas, and the prehistory of bathing" *Antiquity* 61, 370-379.

Barfield, L.H. 1991, "Hot stones: hot food or hot baths?" in Hodder, M.A. And Barfield L.H. *Burnt Mounds and Hot Stone Technology* Sandwell Metropolitan Borough Council, Sandwell 59-67.

Buckley, V. (Compiler) 1990, *Burnt Offerings: International Contributions to Burnt Mound Archaeology,* Wordwell Academic Publications, Dublin,

Calder, C.S.T. 1956 Report on the discovery of numerous Stone Age house-sites in Shetland. *Proceedings of the Society of Antiquaries of Scotland* LXXXIX (1955-56), 340-397.

Calder, C.S.T. 1963. Cairns, Neolithic houses and burnt mounds in Shetland. *Preceedings of the Society of Antiquaries of Scotland* XCVI (1962-63), 37-86.

Dockrill, S.J. and Gater, J.A. 1992.Tofts Ness: Exploration and Interpretation in a Prehistoric Landscape, in Spoerry, P. (ed) *Geoprospection in the Archaeological Landscape*. Oxbow Monograph 18, Oxford. 25-31.

Dockrill, S. J. 1992. *The South Nesting Palaeolandscape Project: Report on 1991 Fieldwork*. Archaeological Sciences, University of Bradford.

Dockrill, S.J., Bond, J.M.,Milles, A., Simpson, I. and Ambers J. 1994 "Tofts Ness, Sanday, Orkney. An integrated study of a buried Orcadian landscape." in Luff, R. and Rowley-Conwy (eds) *Whither Environmental Archaeology?* Oxbow Monograph 38. Oxford

Dockrill S.J. and Simpson I.A., 1994 "The Identification of Prehistoric Anthropogenic Soils In The Northern Isles Using an Integrated Sampling Methodology". *Archaeological Prospection*, Volume 1 Number 2 (1994) 75-92.

Ferguson, L, 1990, Appendix 2: A Gazetteer of burnt mounds in Scotland, in Buckley, V *Burnt Offerings: International Contributions to Burnt Mound Archaeology* Wordwell Ltd — Academic Publications. Dublin.

Hedges, J. 1977. Excavation of two Orcadian burnt mounds at Liddle and Beaquoy, *Proceedings of the Society of Antiquaries of Scotland* 106 (1974-75), 39-98.

Hodder, M.A. And Barfield L.H. 1991, *Burnt Mounds and Hot Stone Technology* Sandwell Metropolitan Borough Council, Sandwell

Henshall, A. 1963 *The Chambered Cairns of Scotland Vol.1* Edinburgh University Press, Edinburgh.

Hunter, J.R. and Dockrill, S.J. 1990. Recent research into burnt mounds on Fair Isle, Shetland and Sanday, Orkney, in Buckley, V. (Compiler) *Burnt Offerings: International Contributions to Burnt Mound Archaeology,* Wordwell Academic Publications, Dublin, 62-68.

Jeffery, S. 1991, "Burnt mounds, fulling and early Textiles" in Hodder, M.A. And Barfield L.H. *Burnt Mounds and Hot Stone Technology*, Sandwell Metropolitan Borough Council, Sandwell 97-107.

Mykura, W 1976. *British Regional Geology: Orkney and Shetland,* Her Majesty's Stationery Office, Edinburgh.

Øvrevik, S. 1990, "The Second Millennium and After" in Renfrew, C. *The Prehistory of Orkney* , 2nd Edition, Edinburgh University Press, Edinburgh 131-149.

LANDSCAPE AND LIFE IN GLETNESS AND RAILSBROUGH, SOUTH NESTING, IN HISTORICAL TIMES

R. Leask, A. K. Bradley & J. M. Bradley

Historical times amount to a far shorter time span than the prehistoric period which preceded them. Although covering historical times as a whole, much of the information for this paper derives from the more recent past, i.e. the 18th and 19th centuries. In addition, it is not just the span of time that is restricted; to write in a meaningful manner on the material covered by our title has required us to centre our study on a limited area. We plan to concentrate on Gletness and Railsbrough, two small townships, and their associated scattald and additional common land in the southernmost part of South Nesting (fig 40).

There is every reason to believe that Gletness and Railsbrough are typical of the other parts of South Nesting and that, by studying them, insights into the wider area can be achieved. We have neither the space nor the knowledge to paint a complete historical picture but have used physical remains, oral accounts and published material to build up a comment on life over the last few hundred years.

Settlement Changes in Time

Both Railsbrough and Gletness are ancient settlements packed with evidence of prehistoric occupation. Evidence of habitation and former cultivation is also to be found on higher ground when a more favourable climate prevailed than has been the case in more recent times.

The roots of crofting go back to a very early period. Fertile coastal sites would probably have been settled first but, in response to pressure on land, pasture was carved out of rough grassland at ever-higher altitudes, e.g. Swaefeld (fig 40). Swaefeld may represent a kind of prehistoric 'ootset' and could have been the last prehistoric structure to be built in the area and the first to be abandoned. Early crofts were patches of cultivated land surrounded by dykes outside which were areas of grazing.

By the height of the Norse period due to continual pressure on land all the best sites were cultivated (Nicolson, 1978) and higher, more marginal sites had to be put under the plough. The name Da Daals (fig 40) indicates a patch of either arable or grass land and is found high in the Gletness hill. Finnister (fig 40), also in the hill, is possibly named after a special type of grass, (*Nardus stricta*), which maintains a particularly green sward (Stewart, 1987, p237).

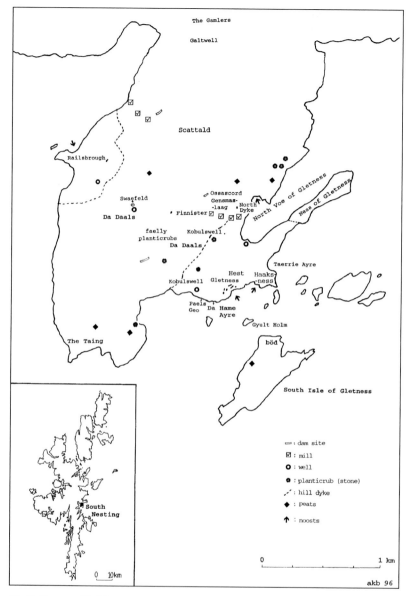

Fig 40. Gletness and Railsbrough location map.

84

During Norse times a system known as runrig developed, which involved tenants holding land in a number of rigs or strips scattered amongst those of their neighbours (Fenton, 1978). These rigs lay between the hill dyke (which divided rough hill pasture from arable land and good grassland) and the township, and were separated one from another only by ditches or ridges (Nicolson, 1978). Beyond the township the landscape must have appeared open. In fact the late Geordie Gear (local historian) spoke of John Sutherland of Gletness and his four sons dragging a large sixareen from the North Voe of Gletness to the Hame Ayre of South Gletness (fig 40) in 1776, unhindered by dykes, a feat which would not have been possible at the end of the nineteenth century.

Settlement in this area subsequently retreated to the coastal locations, Railsbrough and Gletness. The coastal township of Gletness was known as 'Hame Gletness' or 'Da Hooses', and was composed of closely-related households. In the 1804 Meal Distribution Census, of the eight households in Gletness there were five families of Gears and three families of Pottingers — a close community indeed!

When land pressure reasserted itself in the nineteenth century modern ootsets (an ootset was a small area of land taken in from the scattald, with the laird's permission) were established, e.g. at Finnister, which was taken in by Jeremiah Gear in the 1830s. Two of Jeremiah's daughters were later responsible for building about 800 metres of dry stone dyke which enclose Finnister to this day. Similarly William Robertson was given permission to create an ootset on rocky land at North Dyke in the 1870s. An ootset did not always constitute a full croft and an indication of how difficult it was to scratch a living is provided by the fact that the inhabitants of Finnister cut corn and raised potatoes at Brough, more than 3 kms away, carrying everything home on their backs.

The large number of ootsets in Nesting as a whole meant that there were more people in proportion to the rental land than any other Shetland parish, with the population increasing by 16% between 1801 and 1841. The laird was keen to create ootsets because the resultant rise in population increased the number of fishermen available to bring in income for him. It was the rapid increase in the number of ootsets allied to fractionation in the townships that did most to change the settlement pattern.

In addition to crofts and ootsets there were also cottars' houses which were often built by the men of the township, on the orders of the laird, for less fortunate families. A temporary cottar's house was built in this way for William Robertson near the north Gletness well before he was given permission to take in the North Dyke ootset. A small 4m x 3m cottar house built by the men of Gletness for a widow, Barbara Leask, and her daughter in the 1870s still stands in reasonable condition to this day (fig 41). Barbara Leask was taken off for the day by the men of Gletness and left to fish from skerries for sillocks (coalfish in their first year) until she was picked up in the evening by the men returning from the fishing. She also had the right to keep a cow on the Ness of Gletness. Despite this help Barbara Leask would still have been dependent on the goodwill of neighbours, virtually destitute themselves, who allowed her the use of small plots in the locality.

85

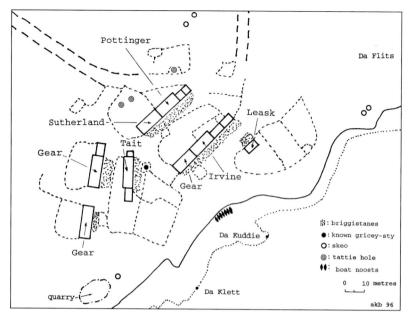

Fig 41. Mid 19th Century Hame Gletness (Da Hooses).

The Organisation of the Crofting Life

Despite good arable and grass land on the fertile limestone soils in the Gletness-Railsbrough area it was said of Nesting in 1793 that "The agriculture is in the same wretched state as that in all the Shetland Islands. The people direct their sole attention to the fishing, and consider the cultivation of the land as only a secondary object" (Sinclair, ed. 1799) which was to be expected, given the laird's demands on his tenants to fish for him.

    This invariably meant that the burden of croft work, as well as its responsibility, fell to the women and children. The younger members of the family were constantly engaged in carrying turf from the hills, seaweed from the shore, water from the wells, breaking up the greens, etc. Everything had to be carried on their backs as there were no roads or bridges. Women looked after children, cooked and washed and, in addition, ran the crofts in the absence of their fishermen husbands. Evidence of this is provided, for example, in two court cases in 1852 involving the harvesting of seaweed in which a large number of the Gletness and Railsbrough women were cited. Women were immured in the chores of crofting, applying themselves in innumerable ways every day of their lives, their contribution to the survival of the family unit incalculable. It is small wonder that an observant old crone, who noted that a young wife's face was paler and more

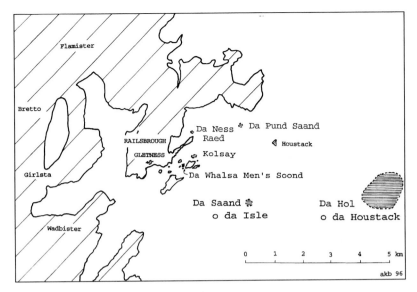

Fig 42. Inshore Fishing grounds off the south Nesting coast.

drawn than usual, is reputed to have said "My joy, du haes tae wirk laek a horse aa week and dan dey lippen dee tae be a mare at da helly!".

Each croft had part of the inbye land, part of the outfield, a few acres of outbait for the summer grazing of sows, a share in a hay meadow and a right in the scattald, a right that they had possessed for many centuries. In Gletness there were two additional features. Each crofter from the township had a right in the common land at the Ness of Gletness (fig 40). Whereas a number of crofters from several townships would have rights in the same scattald, use of the Ness was restricted to Gletness residents alone. In addition, as O'Dell (1939) records, the Gletness crofters rotated the occupancy of six to seven holms and islands every year. This was one of the last cases in Shetland of rotating occupancy, equivalent to true runrig in principle. Geordie Gear always maintained that Gletness folk had greater experience with the sea than any other township in Nesting. In fact he used to say that "Da Gletness lasses could haandle a boat laek a man". This accomplishment was almost certainly connected with the use made of the holms and isles of Gletness.

A number of crofting activities were carefully regulated. For example, sheep could not be rooed (plucked) until the baillie said so (Donaldson, ed. 1991), by the 15 April dykes had to be repaired, no swine or sheep were permitted in the hill before that date and no horses were permitted before 1 May. No floss (common rush) could be cut before Lammas Day (12 August). Railsbrough and Gletness residents had to travel to Flamister and Bretto (fig 42), several kilometres distant, to cut floss for making simmonds (rope), with the result that it was an all-day activity.

Bere (*Hordeum vulgare*) was the main crop in the time before the breakdown in the system of communal farming. Cultivation of bere had, however, almost ceased by the 1840s and its place was taken by oats, (*Avena strigosa*) (Fenton, 1978).

Trough querns, saddle querns and knockin stanes (examples of which have been found at Hame Gletness) would have been used to grind and de-husk bere in early times. They were still in use until relatively recently, especially when meal ran short and small quantities were required, and when the water mills were not operating, during the summer months.

The process of reducing corn to meal through thrashing, winnowing, kiln-drying and grinding is well known. There is evidence of at least ten water-mills in the area, with the remains of an accompanying dam and sluice present at three of them (fig 40). The earliest mention of a water-mill in Shetland was in 1431 and pertained to a group of townships in Delting. When, in the 1860s, a large commercial mill at nearby Girlsta (fig 42) was established, all the corn from a wide area was taken there for drying and grinding. Whalsay men took corn to Girlsta, choosing to shorten their journey by negotiating a narrow and shallow sound between Tainga Skerry and the North Isle of Gletness, thus giving rise to the name, Da Whalsa Men's Soond (fig 42).

Potatoes were first introduced to Shetland in 1730 (O'Dell, 1939) and it was not long before they became the staple food of Shetland, supplementing the traditional diet of fish. Despite diseases in the mid-nineteenth century and the perennial problem of early frosts and snow, the Crofters Commission (Napier Commission, 1884) reported that "people trust more their potatoes than their corn for their living". Potatoes were kept in tattie holes (fig 41) and later in tattie hooses, purpose-built turf-covered structures, and later still in tattie crös, which were all designed to preserve the crop over the cold, wet winter months.

Every household would also have a skeo (a rough stone structure built in an exposed place to catch the wind) for the preservation of perishables, mainly fish (fig 41). The marked skeo sites were later re-used as tattie holes. Donaldson (1991) records criminal action taken against Mans Christopherson of Garth, South Nesting who "under silence and cloud of night" broke into Turvell Ollason's skeo at Gletness and stole a number of codlings in the winter of 1627.

In 1808 the Rev. Turnbull introduced the first turnips into Shetland and thirty years later they were being used throughout the isles. Cabbage too, in the form of kale, increased in importance in the nineteenth century. By the 1850s some families were planting 3,000 kale plants for their own consumption and for their animals, particularly cattle.

Kail plants were started in planticrubs (walled enclosures). Originally these would have been built of turf and the remains of faelly (turf) planticrubs can still be seen in the Gletness hill (fig 40). Later planticrubs were built of stone, making use of the convenient supply of stone from some ancient structure. Consequently their siting was often random. Similarly, stone dykes replaced faelly dykes during the second half of the nineteenth century.

Nicolson (1978) gives an excellent breakdown of the crofting calendar of 100 years ago, touched on below, and we can assume that similar timings would have applied to the Gletness-Railsbrough area.

The crofting cycle commenced during the depths of winter. Waar (the broad-leafed seaweed *Fucus digitatus*) was used as manure on a wide scale. Heavy seas broke the growth free and threw it into large heaps on the beaches. The crofters would then, working collectively, fork it into kishies and carry it clear of the shore where it was dumped to form a midden and was later divided among them. Places along the shore where seaweed washed up often carry the prefix 'taerrie' e.g. the beach, Taerrie Ayre, at Gletness (fig 40).

Burning heather constituted one of the first activities of voar (spring) and was carried out before 11 April so that the bird-nesting was unaffected. In early April the voar work began in earnest. The land had to be delled by use of the labour-intensive Shetland spade. Potatoes were set first. Oats had to be sown by Simmermill Day, 25 April, bere was sown in May, peats were cut and the sheep lambed. In early May the haaf (deep-sea) fishing began, thus leaving all croftwork to women and to children. If bere was beginning to shoot at Johnsmas (24 June) this would be a sign of an early hairst (harvest). Hentilagets (bits of wool lying in the parks) were collected by the poor, and the sheep would be caaed for rooin. In August the hay was cut and cured, early potatoes were lifted and the men returned from the haaf fishing.

In September the oats and bere were ready and the corn harvested and carried in (gorhirded). In October the main potato crop was lifted. Hairst was crucial to every crofting family's existence. Stock from the hill could now roam freely on the rigs. It was not long before winter descended again.

Peat was the main source of fuel. Peats were cut just before the haaf fishing started but the drying process was mainly organised by the women and children. Never idle, the women would walk to and from the peat hill, kishie (straw basket) on their backs and knitting some small garment, sock or glove, as they went, fingers flying. The crofters from Hame Gletness took their peats from the Taing (fig 40), the South Isle of Gletness and latterly from Wadbister (fig 42) from whence peats were flitted by boat. The Robertsons of North Dyke took their peats from nearby Ossascord and Gensmaslaag (fig 40). Railsbrough and Finnester folk cut their peats above Swaefeld.

Animals on the Croft

Peat also had a use for the animals. Hamilton (1954) describes byres at Clickimin Broch overlain by a fibrous peaty material spread as bedding for cattle in winter, since straw had more valuable uses. The same system was used right down the centuries and the remains of several møldi-kus (a stone-ringed base where fibrous peat was collected), and evidence of møldi-bletts (denuded areas from which this fibre had been scraped), can be seen around the summit of The Gamlers (fig 40).

Having been left to dry all summer the møld was carried home by kishie and stored in a corner of the byre to be used as bedding as required. Eventually, when soiled, it was put out on the midden to be used later as manure. Peat-stack debris was also used as bedding.

Norse names and place-names provide us with a useful insight into the use of land for animals in the Gletness-Railsbrough area in former times. There are two instances of the use of the place-name Kobulswell (raised area on which cattle bed down, or böl) in Gletness (fig 40).

But perhaps pride of place belongs to pigs. Each part of Shetland carries a nickname for its inhabitants, e.g. a Lerwick Whiting, and people who came from Nesting would be referred to as a Nesting Gaat (a castrated boar)! This might well suggest that pigs were more common in Nesting than elsewhere in Shetland. Most crofts in Gletness-Railsbrough would have had their own pig(s) and the location of one old gricey-sty (pig-sty) is remembered to this day (fig 41). In addition Gyult Holm (fig 40) was also known as Swinholm (pig island), this latter name being recorded as being in use in 1790 (Stewart, 1987). Galtwell provides a third place-name reference to pigs (fig 40).

Sheep were also an important part of the local economy and mutton would have figured prominently in the local inhabitants' diet. The wool was essential for clothing for the family, and in earlier times part of the rent and taxation was paid in wadmel, a coarsely woven cloth. Geese, ducks and hens would also have been kept.

The Role of Fishing

There were two main types of fishing undertaken; fishing for subsistence and fishing forced on the able men by the laird (the haaf, or ocean, fishing).

The subsistence fishing consisted mainly of piltocks (coalfish, *Gadus virens*, which were between two and four years old) and sillocks. These were fished all year round, whenever the weather allowed. When the able-bodied men were away at the haaf fishing subsistence fishing fell to old men and young boys. Virtually every household had a small boat, each with its own noost (figs 40, 41), some still visible today.

When the wind was too strong to allow a small boat to engage in subsistence fishing the alternative was often angling by waand (rod) from a rock or ledge giving access to a deep pool where sillocks abound. These rocks are known as kraeg saets and had individual names e.g. Da Klett and Da Kuddie at Gletness (fig 40). Paels Geo (fig 40) suggests the presence of a rock ledge and no doubt some outcrop here served as a kraeg saet. There are others in Gletness e.g. at the Taerrie Ayre, and at Railsbrough.

The bait was not fixed to the hooks but consisted of chewing up limpets (soe) or chopping them in soen hols then spröin (spitting) them on the sea to create an oily sheen (löm) on the water to attract sillocks and other fish. Popular sites are indicated by soen hols where repeated generations had been chopping limpets with a stone thus carving out bowl-shaped hollows, as can be seen on Da Klett, the principal kraeg saet at Gletness.

Occasionally men had the opportunity to drive whales, particularly caain (pilot) whales, on to the shore. The laird had the right to demand one third of the kill and part of the remainder was used by the crofters, primarily for blubber as the flesh was not eaten.

It was the laird-tenant relationship of the haaf fishing that rendered almost every able-bodied, adult male a virtual slave of the laird. The men had to fish for the laird under pain of eviction. The old men and young boys helped to cure the catch. On the South Isle of Gletness a fishing böd (fig 40) was built on the site of an ancient structure. The böd has since been modified to serve as a crö for sheep.

Economic depression in the late seventeenth century led to the lairds becoming fish-buyers and they in turn introduced the sub-division of land, with the result that holdings became too small to support a family.

For generations haddock and whiting had been taken from places such as Da Saand o da Isle, Da Hol o da Houstack and Da Pund Saand (fig 42). A variety of fish were caught at Da Ness Raed and piltocks at Kolsay. For many years the sheltered Pund Saand was the exclusive preserve of the laird; any tenant caught fishing there faced eviction. From about 1750, for 150 years men fished for ling, tusk and cod at the Far Haaf, up to 65 km from land.

The haaf season lasted from mid-May to mid-August and while ashore men lived in rough stone-walled lodges while they cured their catch. Occasionally a terrible price was paid in lives lost. In July 1832 105 men were lost, 42 of them from neighbouring Lunnasting and from Whalsay. Francis Pottinger (b. 1786) of Gletness was a haaf skipper and his boat was one of the relatively few to survive. It was the rapid rise of the herring industry from the 1870s onwards which brought the haaf fishing to an end. By 1884 there were two first-class sail-driven herring drifters at Gletness owned by Gletness men. During winter they were anchored in sheltered Catfirth. The boom was over by the time of World War I.

Population Changes

Epidemics of smallpox occurred until about 1740 and other infectious diseases also took their toll. There were also regular fishing disasters when able-bodied men lost their lives. In addition the consequences of the activities of the Press Gang should not be underestimated. Men-of-War intercepted haaf boats and pressed their crews into service. In the nearby Skellister Hill there is a place where a hole (known as Da Dunder Hol) has been cut out of the peat so that men could hide from the Press Gang. Instead of taking the one hundred men each county was expected to provide,

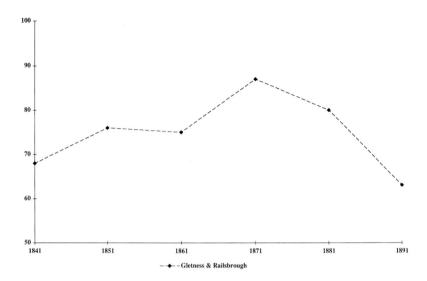

Fig 43. Population changes, Gletness and Railsbrough 1841 – 1891.

Shetland probably had about 5,000 men serving in 1815. These men were away for a considerable period of time and a substantial number never returned.

It was considered at the time of the Napoleonic Wars that Shetland could produce only one third of the meal required to feed its population. The balance had to be imported and paid for by the produce of the haaf fishing and crofts as well as from cottage industry. When the Press Gang starting abducting the haaf boat crews, the fishing was virtually reduced to a standstill and hunger to the point of starvation was in many cases the result. People were driven to the ebb to seek shellfish and edible seaweed such as hinnywaar (*Alaria esculenta*) and dulse (*Rhodymenia palmata*). Widespread starvation occurred in the months March - May in 1803 and 1804, when oatmeal ran out. Quakers in England sent relief to Shetland, with families in Gletness and Railsbrough benefiting.

From the mid-eighteenth century population began to increase rapidly, with Shetland reaching its peak in the 1860s. With no security of tenure and the confiscation of scattald in some areas (though not Gletness-Railsbrough) to boost the laird's sheep numbers, emigration was the inevitable result. It would appear that Gletness and Railsbrough peaked in 1871-81 (fig 43) later than the rest of Shetland, but by 1891 the effects of emigration were becoming evident there too. At this time North America attracted a number of young people for example, Pottingers from Railsbrough and many Gletness residents too. Quite a number of the Gletness Gears moved to the colonies: New Zealand, Australia and South Africa.

92

Changes in Crofting Legislation

In 1883 the teacher at the South Nesting School and Inspector of the Poor represented Nesting to the Crofters' Commission hearing. The chief causes of complaint were high rents (which had doubled over the previous 30 years), lack of security of tenure, lack of compensation for improvements, lack of roads, inferior quality of dwellings, and the laird's claim to a share of whales captured.

Nesting had suffered at the hands of the laird of Symbister. In 1797 a considerable number of South Nesting folk were evicted. That same year the residents of Gletness received notice of eviction but they must have managed to stave it off as they were all recorded as present in 1804.

The laird later had taken a piece of the Gletness-Railsbrough scattald, but it was only a small portion. The Crofters' Act gave the crofter security of tenure, the right to compensation for improvements and the right to assign his holding to a member of his family. Many lairds then ceased to take an interest in their tenants since they no longer had any control over their property, except the right to collect rent.

The geography of Gletness settlement changed. With the exception of two ootsets, originally all the crofthouses were grouped together at Hame Gletness. After the Crofting Acts, however, a number of new crofthouses were built on the crofters' own land. James o da Ness (James Gear) was the first to resite his dwelling house in the 1880s. He was followed by William Irvine, and the last to do so was Willie Tait in 1928.

The next major effect on the crofting scene occurred at the end of the First World War. A whole generation of young men had been wiped out and some lairds had suffered financially too. The Symbister estate, like others in Shetland, was prepared to sell crofts to tenants who had the wherewithal to pay the equivalent of 25 years' rent. Many tenants were precluded from doing so but some crofters managed to buy and there were examples of men who had emigrated to America and were pleased to find a use for money they had earned during the war years. Thus one Railsbrough exile and his sister was able to buy a Railsbrough croft from under the nose of the sitting tenant.

Conclusion

Throughout this paper there is a sense of continuity. Although there were fundamental changes in the latter part of the nineteenth century, the way of life enjoyed — or otherwise — by the inhabitants of Gletness and Railsbrough had varied little over a long period of time.

Perhaps the most exciting aspect is the survival of some features which were in existence before the dawn of history. Peat møld was used as animal bedding at broch sites and right up to the end of the last century, kraeg saets that are probably just as old are still in use today, and until the 1960s water was still being drawn from the well at the ancient site of Swaefield high in the Gletness hill, when the two township wells ceased to function in dry summers.

Since crofting times, in the recent past, change has been rapid but there are still examples of evidence pointing to an intriguing way of life in past centuries to be found if you look for it, and more importantly, if you know where to look for it. We have examined two small townships within a small area; similar studies of other parts of the islands would contribute to the rich tapestry of Shetland local history, complementing its rich archaeological past.

Acknowledgments

This account has been inspired by one man in particular — Geordie o Lingness (George Gear, latterly of Eswick). We had been privileged to learn about the past 250 years or so from this humble man with a computer-like recall of the past. Sadly he died on New Year's Day 1996. While writing this paper there were numerous occasions when we said "If only we could ask Geordie". We are also grateful to Brian Smith, Archivist, who gave of his limited time to provide invaluable guidance. We would also like to thank local residents, particularly of Gletness, for their help.

References

Donaldson, G. (ed.), 1991 *Court Book of Shetland 1615-1629*. Lerwick.

Fenton, A. 1978 *The Northen Isles: Orkney and Shetland*. Edinburgh.

Hamilton, J.R.C. 1954 *Excavations at Clickhimmin, Shetland*. HMSO, Edinburgh

Napier Commission. 1884 *Evidence taken by Her Majesty's Commission of Inquiry into the condition of the Crofters and Cottars in the Highlands & Islands of Scotland*. Parliamentary Papers, Volume II pp. 848 - 1696, Edinburgh

Nicolson, J.R. 1978 *Traditional Life in Shetland*. London

O'Dell, A.C. 1939 *This Historical Geography of the Shetland Islands*. Lerwick.

Sinclair, Sir J. Ed. (1799). *The Statistical Account of Scotland 1791 - 1799: Volume XIX Orkney and Shetland*. Wakefield.

Stewart, J. 1987. *Shetland Place-names*. Lerwick.

VIKINGS ON THE HILLSIDE AT CATPUND, CUNNINGSBURGH

Val Turner

The geological softness of steatite (or soapstone) was known and used by people living in Shetland as long ago as the Neolithic period (about 5000 years ago). Being a very soft rock, it was easy to crush up and mix with clay in order to temper the pot (stop it shrinking and cracking on firing). Steatite is found in prehistoric pottery from sites all over Shetland, but it is less common to find large numbers of objects made from it. The techniques of making vessels from the stone were known in prehistoric times however, and there are two large bronze age cinerary urns, found in Orkney, in the Tankerness House Museum. By way of contrast, it is rare to find Viking pottery on archaeological sites, and that which does exist is poor in quality. Instead, the Vikings used natural materials in order to create vessels and plates. A lot of this does not survive, being of wood or skins, but the Viking settlers to Shetland used steatite to manufacture vessels on a far larger scale than had been done before.

Catpund, Cunningsburgh, in the South Mainland of Shetland, has long been known as a source of this soapstone, but the extent of the Catpund workings had remained a mystery. When Hamilton excavated the Viking levels at Jarlshof, he found "large quantities of steatite....As no outcrop of this rock occurred in the immediate vicinity, and as there was an almost total absence of chips and wasters, it was apparent that the objects had been imported ready made..." (Hamilton, 1956, 206). Catpund is the closest source of steatite to Jarlshof, and so in 1951 Hamilton initiated an examination of the burn. He located 15 spoil heaps, two of which he put trial trenches across and he identified three types of bowls which were made there.

In 1986, within three weeks of the author having taken up the newly created post of Shetland Archaeologist, it became clear that a minerals extraction company, operating under the name of "Shetland Talc", had already carried out testing in the area and was anxious to proceed in gaining planning permission. The author could see the potential for commercial and historical interests to exist side by side, but in order to achieve this, it was necessary to embark on a programme of detailed archaeological survey and targeted excavation.

What is Steatite?

"Steatite", "soapstone" and, in Shetland dialect, "clebber" are all common names for a soft ultrabasic talcose rock. Its mineral components can vary, but Shetland soapstone is a mixture of hydrous magnesium silicate (talc) and smaller quantities

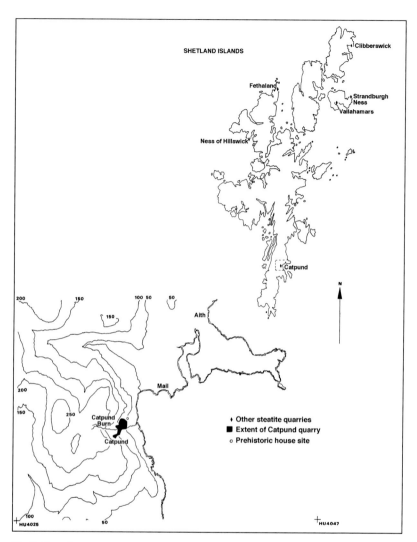

Fig 44. The major sources of steatite in Shetland.

of carbonates chlorate, amphibole and opaque minerals, formed by the hydrothermal metamorphism of serpentinite. (Mykura 1976).

The largest sources of steatite in the western world occur in Norway, with other sources being Sweden, Greenland, Newfoundland and of course elsewhere in Shetland. There are also small outcrops in Dumfries, Harris, Anglesey, the Lizard Peninsula and in Ireland, but there is no evidence of any of these ever having been worked during antiquity (Ritchie 1984). There are five known sources of worked steatite within Shetland: Fethaland, North Mainland; Clibberswick, Unst; Valhammars and Strandibrough in Fetlar, and Catpund (fig 44). A pink type of steatite also occurs at Hillswick, in the North Mainland and a fragmented of very rotten pink steatite found during the 1997 excavations at Bayanne, Yell, indicates that perhaps this too was once worked. There is so much variation in mineral content at each Shetland source that attempts to identify the origins of pieces found on archaeological sites has not been achieved using scientific methods (Buttler and Moffat 1986). At the moment the best way of identifying the source of any given piece of steatite is by looking at it!

The Investigation

The extent of the steatite seams at Catpund had already been investigated by the Institute of Geological Sciences (1970 -71), Roy Ritchie, Historic Scotland (1984), and by Charles Morley of Shetland Talc (1986). They had identified three seams which were close to the surface on the north side of the burn, but dipped down to the south. How much of this had been known to people in Viking times and previously?

In 1987 and 1988, the author undertook a detailed topographical survey of the hillside. She was assisted in this by Alison Innes, Jane Mack and the Shetland Archaeological Survey Group, an amateur group who learnt to survey and helped with the project during the light evenings of 1987.

The survey was followed up with a series of small excavations, each targeted to answer specific questions. The quarries are scheduled, and the Historic Buildings and Monuments Department (now Historic Scotland) were anxious that the excavations should be confined to the area which stood to be affected by the modern quarry. As a result, the excavations which took place were all either close to the burn, or to the north of it, and there was no opportunity to examine the southern end of the quarries where the nature of both the steatite and the method of working may be different.

The excavations took place over two seasons; in 1988 Beverley Ballin Smith excavated a prehistoric house site and Stephen Carter opened a spoil heap which was located at the foot of a worked outcrop beside the burn. In 1990 Jamie Hamilton examined a number of small sites within the quarry. Paul Sharman was present on both occasions and undertook an analysis of the tool marks and methods

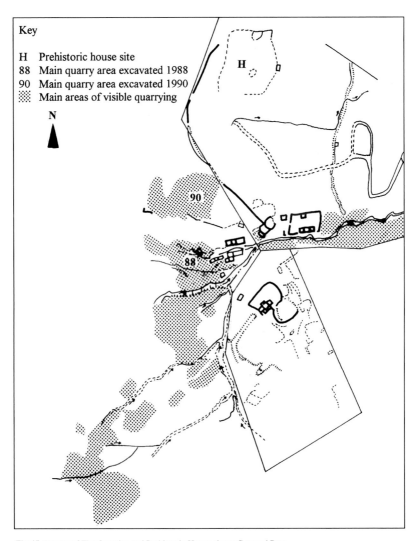

Key

H   Prehistoric house site
88   Main quarry area excavated 1988
90   Main quarry area excavated 1990
▓   Main areas of visible quarrying

N

Fig 45. Survey of The Quarries and Prehistoric House site at Catpund Burn.

of manufacture, both on site and subsequently in the laboratory. The details of this work are nearing publication, and the purpose of this paper is to provide an overview of how the hillside was used.

The Quarries

All along Catpund burn there were areas of worked rock visible as hollows of either square or round shape. These were the result of using chisels to cut around the edge of a block of the appropriate size and then prizing it off the live rock. Catpund Burn flowed over some of the worked surfaces, other surfaces were situated adjacent to the burn. Large natural outcrops also showed signs of working, and we wondered if the burn had been diverted deliberately in places, using the quarry waste as a barrier across the original course of the burn. We imagined that the purpose of diverting the burn would be in order to expose new areas of stone which could be worked, and there were certainly places where the course of the burn clearly had altered as a result of the deposition of spoil in earlier times.

To the south of the burn there were extensive spoil heaps, which were ranged around roughly oval shaped flat areas. Roy Ritchie suggested that these may represent shafts which had been sunk into the hillside in order to mine the steatite where the layers dipped more deeply (Ritchie 1984). This type of mining had been carried out in Østre Myre, Vegarshei in Norway where there are pits up to 7m deep (Skjølsvold, 1961). Other Catpund hollows have spoil downslope from them, and may also represent mine shafts. There also appear to be flat platforms dug into the rock.

The worked area to the south of the burn occupies a natural bowl, created by the surrounding hills. The spoil heaps in this area have slopes of up to 60° and are unstable, but as a result are free draining. Little soil has formed on them and the plant cover is incomplete. Stephen Carter (1989) identified the vegetation cover as being mainly of grasses, sedges, thyme, sea plantain and moss campion. On the more stable slopes and on level areas, he identified a species rich heath. Some of the flatter areas are poorly drained however, and so the vegetation cover is variable. The area is dissected by drainage channels, and in these Carter identified an alluvium having a high organic content and a sedge peat.

The working tailed off quite close to the burn on its north side, although this was where the steatite was closest to the surface. From this point north, the steatite deposits dip below the surface again (Mining Magazine, July 1986) however there is no suggestion that it had ever been worked further north.

In 1988 we decided to examine a spoil tip from the quarry. This had a worked steatite outcrop above it (to the west). Today the burn runs to the north of the excavated area, but it had once run to the south. The area which was opened up measured 10m x 8m and was supervised by Stephen Carter.

When the spoil heap was excavated to bedrock, we were surprised to find that the bedrock itself had been quarried, and was densely covered in holes from

Fig 46. The freshly uncovered bedrock at the bottom of the quarry.

which blocks for vessels had been extracted. This suggested that quarrying had taken place over the whole hillside, and was not restricted to the areas which are visible along the burn. This helps to explain the large quantity of debris on the hill, which was clearly far too great to have come from the obviously quarried areas. It also means that the steatite "industry" was far bigger than we had previously realised. Along the burn at least, the quarry had been worked in steps of up to 2m in height.

The newly uncovered bedrock contained over 160 holes, which varied from about 0.2m square, to oval holes of up to 0.7m long (fig 46). Within this there appeared to be five discrete areas of working, which may have represented separate quarrying events. There was a northern group of vessel blocks, west and south-west groups of square vessel blocks, a south group of rounded and/or rectangular blocks and an east group of plates and square vessel blocks. This suggested a measure of organisation within this restricted area of the quarry.

The spoil heaps which were excavated contained two discrete heaps, the earliest of which seems to be the result of working the quarry floor. The top of this early heap was probably the result of extracting vessels from the surviving cuts which were found on the quarry floor. There was 2-3m of spoil above the surface of this quarry heap which contained steatite rubble within a fine matrix of steatite. The steatite was not heavily compacted and so the heap was free draining at the top. The lowest levels of the slope which we opened up were waterlogged, and so the quarry floor was not uncovered across the entire area. The cuts in the floor were probably

100

covered up almost as soon as they were created, the result of removing the adjacent block. Most of the sockets looked very fresh, and were full of clean, sharp, uncontaminated, debris.

Once this phase of working had ended, a peaty soil developed. Camilla Dickson examined two samples from the peat and found that rushes, heather and grasses were abundant. There were two grains present which may have been barley, together with only a trace of arable weeds. Sphagnum indicated locally boggy ground and there were also indications of short grass. There was very little tree pollen present; the birch, hazel willow and alder pollen may have been local, but the pollen from pine, oak and elm had probably travelled a long distance (Dickson, 1989).

Later, spoil accumulated on the area again as a result of quarrying the step above. The southern edge of the spoil heap had slumped into the stream to the south and had apparently become mixed up by it. A wall had been built on top of the spoil heap, perhaps to provide shelter between it and the rock face. When the burn changed course, it washed both spoil and part of the wall away. Peat began to form again, on top of the second pile of spoil, but Camilla Dickson found that the vegetation had changed very little, apart from a lack of willow and elm pollen in the later peat.

The debris in the spoil heap consisted of waste from the quarrying process, together with half finished broken vessels and plates, plate and vessel blanks and blocks, and waste. (A block is the piece of rock which has been removed from the quarry floor; a blank has been shaped externally but not yet hollowed out.) A smoothing stone and a few sandstone whetstones were also found among the debris, but otherwise no quarry tools were found. Similarly, there were no small artefacts found, and it would appear that spindle whorls, netsinkers, loomweights, etc were manufactured away from the quarry. Indeed, none of the vessels which were found had been finished, and it would seem that once the Norse people had cut the rough shape and hollowed it out, thereby reducing the weight significantly, they took the objects away from the quarry to finish off elsewhere. So far, no finishing areas have been identified anywhere in Shetland.

Paul Sharman has studied the artefacts found in the quarry in some detail, (the results of which will be published shortly) and he has concluded that there is such a wide variation in the methods of tooling and in the shapes and thickness of the vessels, that it is unlikely that the steatite "industry" was organised, or undertaken by a skilled workforce. The variety of shapes was partially determined by the planes of fracture within the stones, and when a vessel broke there was sometimes an attempt to salvage it, by turning it into something else. Sharman suggests that individual people might have had their own area of the quarry, in the same way as Shetlanders have their own peat banks today. This does not necessarily conflict with the apparent local organisation seen within the small area excavated, but it must be remembered that we are only looking at a small part on the fringes at the north end of the quarry, where the quality of the steatite is not high.

Several small trenches were excavated in the north area of the quarry in 1990 (fig 45), supervised by Jamie Hamilton, and two of these helped to shed further light on working practices at the quarry. One of these was a trench opened up over what appeared to be a depression 3m in diameter, in the surface of the hillside, surrounded on three sides by upcast, and by the hillslope on the north, upslope, side. The excavated area was 6m x 2m. The quarry spoil itself was fairly featureless. The pit was roughly stepped to the north, east and south, and was 1.5m deep. On the west side the natural face overhung the pit, and contained few toolmarks. The other faces contained neat, closely spaced toolmarks, made with pointed tools or chisels. There were no vessel cuts in the rock, instead the steatite appeared to have been removed in sub-rectangular blocks of approximately 1m x 0.5m x 0.5m. Later quarrying cut through earlier pits. This quarry was part of a linear outcrop which extended to the south from the site, and may have been exploited by working along a natural plane in the rock; the area which was opened up was too small for us to be certain. This would accord with the east facing rock being the face containing relatively few toolmarks. The excavated spoil contained 254 pieces of freshly tooled steatite, including broken artefacts and freshly tooled pieces. There is a parallel for this type of working at Brennepösen, Akerhus, where there is pit working up to 4m deep (Skjølsvold, 1961).

The fact that this pit did not prove to be a mine shaft does not mean that the depressions to the south are not the tops of mine shafts. Further excavation is needed in order to establish this one way or the other.

Another area of working which was investigated was situated at the foot of the burn, towards the eastern extremity of the outcrop. There were no signs of Norse working here, although the rock face had been chiselled in places and there were vessel workings only 10m away. The tool marks on this rock face were quite different in character to those higher up the burn, these being shallow and flat, approximately 10mm wide x 3mm deep. While this outcrop may have been worked in Norse times, any traces of it had disappeared as a result of 19th and early 20th century working for fire bricks and hearths. This has taken place within living memory. (When steatite is heated it hardens and becomes more durable and less porous, which makes it ideal for such purposes.)

The one period of steatite working which the survey and excavations of the quarry did not identify was the prehistoric. It may be that this was the result of later working, which was on a much larger scale, having destroyed the earlier evidence. Alternatively, prehistoric people may have used an area of the quarry further to the south, outwith the area of visible surface working and excavation. The area along the burn, which formed the subject of out excavations comprised coarse grained steatite, and it is possible that prehistoric people did not have the necessary skill in order to use it. The steatite at some of the other quarries in Shetland, such as Valhammers in Fetlar, is much more finely grained, and so would have been easier to work. It is possible that the steatite at the southern end of the Catpund quarry was less coarse grained, although this has yet to be examined.

The Prehistoric House

To the north of the worked steatite outcrop, at the edge of the cultivable land, there was a prehistoric house within an enclosure. Since steatite was clearly used in prehistoric times, crushed up for tempering pottery, as well as for netsinkers and loom weights and the occasional vessel, we were anxious to know how the house related to the soapstone "industry".

The house (fig 45) was situated a little above 80m above sea level. To the west the land rose steeply, to the east it fell away sharply, with hill terraces below which had been cultivated at some point in the past, and were possibly contemporary. The Burn of Redstane bounded the south side of the enclosure, and there was a second watercourse to the north of the site.

The house lay south-east of the centre of an irregular enclosure. There was also a D-shaped structure against the north face inside the enclosure. To the east a small rectangular structure had been tacked on to the outside of the enclosure, but its double faced construction indicated a much later date than the house site.

Immediately above the site a hilldyke roughly followed the 100m contour, which curved south towards a more recently abandoned farmstead along Catpund Burn. Below the house, on the east side, were the remains of two further hill dykes.

The shape and design of the Catpund house suggest a typical Neolithic/Bronze Age Shetland house, similar to house 1 from Scord of Brouster (dated to 2195 ±70bc, Whittle 1986, 20). Nothing which could provide an absolute date was found from the house which was built on a natural platform, against the break of slope, with the entrance to the south-west. There was a paved area outside the house, which curved to the north-west, and which would have protected the entrance from the wind.

The excavation of the house was supervised by Beverley Ballin Smith, who found nothing inside the house to suggest a close association between it and the local steatite deposits. The floor deposits were shallow however and only survived in the centre of the house. It is possible that the evidence of steatite working may have existed here and been destroyed later, or that the cleaning of the prehistoric house removed the evidence, but were this to be the case, it is surprising that the evidence has been removed so completely. Large numbers of stone tools were found, including 29 ard points and 119 worked stone tools, but there were only 8 fragments of steatite found, which was a somewhat disappointing result.

Once the house was abandoned and became roofless, it may have temporarily reoccupied, but little remained of this phase. Eventually, crofters made use of the remains, building a plantie crub into the centre of the house, using the pillars as supports for the walls.

The wall of the enclosure which surrounded the house, was also investigated. It was constructed from two lines of boulders, with about a metre apart, and had been infilled with smaller stones. When the D-shaped enclosure was added to the main enclosure dyke, the enclosure dyke had been rebuilt. There was nothing to suggest the date at which this took place. A possible spoil heap was visible adjacent to the enclosure wall. This was examined in 1990, but was found to consist of natural slip from higher up the hill. An area which was examined at the foot of the spoil heap, within the enclosure, contained 231 pieces of weathered steatite, 26 of which were tooled. They seem to have come from a steatite outcrop higher up the slope. There was no trace of working on the underlying bedrock.

There were a few terraces of flat land below the house, and it is reasonable to assume that these would have played a significant role in the economy of the people who lived there. The examination of one of these terraces did not, however, provide any evidence of human interference, although 29 ard points were found during the excavation of the house, implying that the ground was cultivated locally.

Houses Along the Burn

There are several houses which lie along the burn, and there have been many phases of settlement involving the use and reuse of available building stone. Some of these have been used during this century as plantiecrubs, but they may have had Norse, or even earlier, origins.

There are four long structures aligned down the slope beside the burn. One of these structures has an additional two roomed building attached. The size, shape and alignment of the rectangular structures lends credence to the late Peter Moar's suggestion that these are Viking in origin (Shetland Museum Index). Later croft houses were usually aligned along the slope. The structure which is furthest to the east is incorporated into a yard, and one of the "rooms" within it is used today as a plantiecrub. This structure has been incorporated into a yard, which also has a small rectangular building on the opposite wall, as well as traces of other earthworks within the dyke. Immediately west of this are the irregular remains of another group of structures, possibly agricultural in function. There are also three small square structures within the group. Simon Buttler dug a test pit inside one of the structures, but found nothing datable within it (pers. comm.). The density of buildings in such an agriculturally poor area is surprising, if the context is Norse. The land was nothing like as rich as that at Jarlshof, nor building stone so plentiful as to suggest this represents a series of rebuildings of one settlement. Perhaps the community here derived its income from the steatite industry.

To the south, on enclosed and improved land, are the remains of a more complex building, set within a yard, and with a second infield attached to the south. There are also two small rectangular structures set apart from the enclosed area, one of which was probably a duckhouse. This complex gives the impression of being relatively high status, and almost certainly later in date than the rectangular structures.

There is little documentary evidence to shed light on this problem. All these structures are visible on the first edition Ordnance Survey map, surveyed in 1878, as being unroofed. The only structure which has apparently altered since 1878 is the one to the east. The hilldykes, now visible as the foundations of fealie (turf built) dykes are shown as being the current field boundaries on the first edition map. Below the head dyke a second fealie dyke, also aligned approximately north - south but ending at the Catpund Burn to the south, is also depicted as being in use.

The Catpund area became uninhabited so early that there is little oral history associated with it. Five legal petitions do give glimpses into the lives of the people who lived along the burn, together with dates which span almost a century of occupation (1771 - 1860). The individuals, who were all defendants, were Halcrows (1771, 1772, 1787) and Tullochs (1855, 1860). The only records in the Old Parish Register relating to Catpund are the marriage of Laurence Tulloch to Marion Halcrow in 1805, and the subsequent births of their three children (Laurence 1810, Peter 1815, and John 1817). In the census of 1841, four adult males were recorded as living at Catpund (all Tullochs, fishermen by trade). Ten years later, two of these remained together with their families, and by 1871, only Thomas Tulloch and his family remained. By 1881 the population of Catpund seemed to have disappeared completely, and from then on the hillside was used primarily for sheep, other than the small scale removal of stone for hearth stones and fire bricks. At the end of 1996, Shetland Talc sold the mineral rights at Catpund to Talc de Luzenac, who are currently investigating the economic viability of 21st century quarrying adjacent to the Viking quarries.

Acknowledgements

The excavation was financed by Historic Scotland (then HBMD) and Shetland Talc, through Shetland Amenity Trust. I would also like to thank all the participants in the project, particularly Beverley Ballin Smith, Stephen Carter, Paul Sharman and Jamie Hamilton.

References

Carter SP, 1989 "Soils and Vegetation" in Smith (ed.) 1989

Dickson C, 1989 "Botany Report" in Smith (ed)1989

Hamilton J, 1991 "*Catpund 1990, Cunningsburgh, Shetland*" unpublished report, Shetland Amenity Trust

Hamilton JRC, 1956 *Excavations at Jarlshof, Shetland*, HMSO, Edinburgh
Mining Magazine, 1986 "*Encouraging Results in the Development of Shetland Talc, U.K.*" (unattributed) July? 1986

Moffat D & Buttler S.J. 1986 "Rare Earth Element Distribution patterns in Shetland Steatite" *Archaeometry*, 28, 1, 101-115

Mykura W, 1976 *British Regional Geology. Orkney and Shetland* , HMSO, Edinburgh

Ritchie PR, 1984 "Soapstone Quarrying in Viking Lands" in Fenton and Palsson H (ed) *The Northern and Western Isles in the Viking World* 59 - 84

Skjølsvold A, 1961 "Klebersteinsindustrien I Vikingetilden" *Universitetsforlaget*, Oslo — Bergen

Sharman P, (forthcoming) in Shetland Steatite monograph

Shetland Archives SC12/6/1771/3

Shetland Archives SC12/6/1772/4

Shetland Archives SC12/6/1787/39

Shetland Archives "*Old Parish Register for Dunrossness, Sandwick and Cunningsburgh*"

Smith BB (ed), 1989, "*Catpund, Cunningsburgh Shetland. Provisional Report and Archive*" unpublished, Shetland Amenity Trust.

TOWNSHIP, 'HOUSE' AND TENANT-HOLDING; THE STRUCTURE OF RUN-RIG AGRICULTURE IN SHETLAND

William P. L. Thomson

It is now a good number of years since I described run-rig at Funzie in Fetlar using a remarkable survey of the township by A.D. Matthewson[1]. His map and associated papers are the most complete record of run-rig we are ever likely to find, since he recorded the names, size, use, value and occupancy of nearly 500 rigs and grazing sections. However, the subsequent discovery of other good surveys led to the realisation that run-rig was rather more varied than I had first supposed. It is not so much a single system as a set of principles and practices which, depending on the circumstances, produced field-systems of quite different degrees of complexity. It also became evident that, far from being static, run-rig was actually in a state of rapid development in the late eighteenth and early nineteenth century.

Run-rig agriculture in Shetland involved three levels of organisation, the township, the 'house' and the tenant-holding. A township can be envisaged as a confederation of 'houses', bound together by an encircling hill-dyke and united by shared interests in unevenly distributed resources such as arable land, grass and meadow-hay. These constituent 'houses', sometimes known as 'farms', might each be occupied by a single tenant, but they were often divided into two, three or more quite distinct tenant holdings. It can be seen that there are problems with terminology since a 'house' in this sense might be several unrelated households, and 'farm' is an equally unsatisfactory term for places which comprised several quite distinct tenancies. Whereas the township itself and the tenant-holding are levels of organisation which are familiar and easily recognised, the multi-tenanted 'house' is less obvious, and in many townships in the late eighteenth and early nineteenth centuries it was already a vanishing unit.

In the period 1750 to 1830 Shetland agriculture was rapidly changing, yet the process had nothing to do with improvement or modernisation, and indeed in most respects the changes were for the worse. Studies of Irish *rundale* (run-rig) by Desmond McCourt[2] show how, given the right circumstances, farms could rapidly dissolve into numerous run-rig tenancies, and at other periods re-emerge into severalty. Among many examples, he quotes a Donegal township of 205 acres which had consisted of two farms, yet within two generations it fractured into 29 holdings lying run-rig in no less than 422 parcels of land[3]. McCourt's description of run-rig as a dynamic system within which rapid changes could take place has direct relevance to Shetland. Pre-Improvement run-rig was not an age-old static pattern of farming as is often supposed. It is true that a certain amount of run-rig had always been present, generating a rich vocabulary to describe rigs of different shapes and sizes, but the intensification which took place between 1750 and 1830 was something new. Not only did a highly complicated, fragmented and dispersed landscape emerge, but there was also a shift from the 'house' to the whole township as the unit within which sharing took place. The decay and disappearance of the 'house', and the emphasis on whole-township organisation, were reflected on the ground by the abandonment of features such as *garths, punds* and *inner dykes* which had previously created systems of internal division.

The Rev. John Morison, minister of Delting, saw these changes as a direct consequence of the landlords' economic policies. In his 1790 *Statistical Account* of the parish he wrote:

> The inhabitants have not been long compelled by their landlords to prosecute the ling fishery; but, since the proprietors thought proper to employ their tenants in that line, it has become an object to have as many men as possible on their grounds. This circumstance has induced them to split the farms, and to make them so small, that there is now, in many instances, four families on a farm which was possessed, twenty or thirty years ago by one[4].

In 1755 there had been 956 people in the parish of Delting; when Mr Morison wrote his account the population had risen to 1,790 and by 1831 it was to reach 2,070, more than double what it had been eighty years earlier. Population pressures brought about the same run-rig proliferation as in pre-famine Ireland. Farm size declined, plough-cultivation was replaced by the spade (the minister noted that there were "not above six ploughs" in the parish[5]), outfield fallowing became increasingly a luxury and immense efforts were expended on the intensive manuring which was necessary to keep land in continuous infield cultivation[6]. Although virtually the entire population engaged in subsistence agriculture, the main effort was directed into commercial fishing, with the men-folk likely to be away at the fishing stations for much of the summer. The result, according to Mr Morison, was that "everything in the farming line must consequently go to wreck"[7].

Much of what I have to say is based on detailed maps of run-rig at Norwick, Unst (1822), Laxobigging, Delting (1827) and Funzie, Fetlar (1829)[8]. Since these maps originated within a seven-year period they can be used to supplement each other, but the three townships also illustrate different stages of a process which was affecting all of them. Laxobigging, despite the Delting minister's comments, was less subject to the pressures of commercial fishing than Norwick and Funzie, both of which were fishing stations. In 1827 Laxobigging was an old-fashioned, poverty-stricken place where traditional patterns were under pressure, but where its 'houses' were still operational; Norwick represents a transitional stage where the 'ghosts' of houses remained, but Funzie had exploded into a new type of run-rig in which 'houses' had disappeared, internal divisions had been abandoned, and dispersal had been carried to its ultimate conclusion.

Laxobigging shows how surprisingly different conditions could exist simultaneously within the same township. This is clearly illustrated by the 'houses' of Hoya, Graven and Laxo, which provide examples of successive degrees of run-

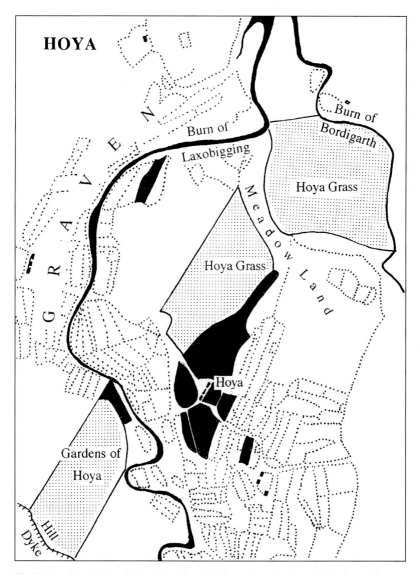

Fig 47. Hoya, Laxobigging. Although Hoya lay within "an antiquated and maze-like landscape", it was a compact farm with one owner and one tenant. It was hardly run-rig at all, apart from the fact that its ultimate definition depended on a a share proportionate to its merks rather than on fixed boundaries. For location within the township, see Fig 49.

rig. (figs 47-49). When the lands of Hoya are plotted it becomes apparent that Hoya was hardly run-rig at all. The 'house' belonged to one proprietor, Arthur Hunter, who let it to one tenant, Magnus Sinclair. Its arable extending to four acres mostly lay in a compact block adjacent to the house. These sections were generally bigger than average, and some had names such as 'flit' and 'broad' which indicate that they were not cultivated in ridged strips. Hoya's grass was not shared with any other proprietor or tenant, and links with other farms were confined to meadowland and to the common grazing outside the hill dyke. Although the farm lay in the heart of an antiquated and maze-like landscape, the term 'run-rig' was hardly applicable, apart from the important proviso that Hoya's ultimate definition depended, not on fixed boundaries, but on 6 merks of land which Hunter held within a 71-merk township[9]. Hoya, despite appearances, was a share rather than an area, and there was always the possibility that, in some future re-organisation, it might disappear, only to be re-created in a new form which might involve greater or lesser degrees of dispersal. An even more likely eventuality was that the proprietor might find another tenant whom he wished to accommodate, and so he might decide to divide the farm. He could easily do so at any time without legal proceedings or other formalities and, if the farm was then run-rig within itself, the new arrangement would not affect the people in Laxobigging's other 'houses'.

At Graven (fig 48) the situation was different. This large 18-merk farm was physically divided from the other farms by a broad tract of grass and meadow, and so Graven was a sub-township, indeed potentially a separate township, with a consolidated block of land nearly as compact as Hoya. It was rented to three tenants, Martha Angus with 4 merks and Andrew Robertson and Archibald Thomson, each with 7 merks. Graven was remarkably close to achieving the run-rig ideal that shares should take into account both the area and the quality of the land. It had been carefully laid out so that the tenants received almost exactly 0.7 acres of arable land for each merk they possessed, and the arable land of all three tenants was in the proportion 46% infield to 54% outfield. In contrast to this exact division, two large tracts of very poor grassland within the hill dykes were held *pro indiviso* (in common) between them.

The three tenants at Graven did not all hold their land from the same laird. Martha Angus was the tenant of James Stout, whereas the other two tenants held their land from Arthur Gifford. As the tenants, or their predecessors, had translated their merks into run-rig, it followed that the 4 merks of James Stout were run-rig with the 14 merks of Arthur Gifford, although neither proprietor is likely to have been involved in the laying-out of the run-rig or indeed to have had the least idea where his land might be found. The lairds' concern was rent; land was the business of the tenants. Proprietorial run-rig of this kind was a form of tenure relatively rare in Scotland, but very common in Shetland because of the complicated inter-mixture of Shetland estates.

There can be no doubt that, for the Graven tenants, their membership of the same 'house' was more important than the fact that they were tenants of different estates, or the fact that they were all members of the bigger unit, the township of Laxobigging. All three tenants lived in a single row of houses along one side of a

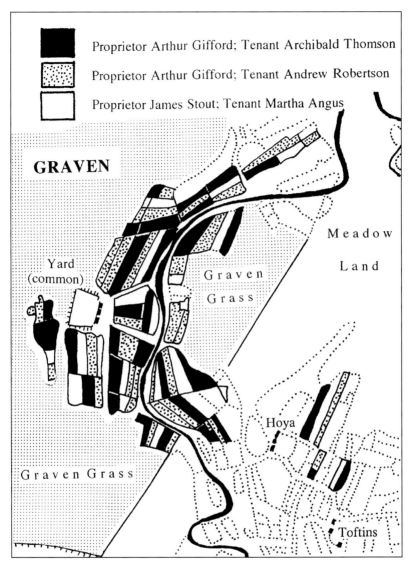

Fig 48. Graven, Laxobigging. Graven was nearly as compact as Hoya (Fig 47), but had two proprietors and three tenants. Thus Graven exhibits both proprietorial run-rig and tenant run-rig which achieved a very precise sharing within the farm according to each person's entitlement.

common yard. All three co-operated for hay-making, and divided the crop in the field. Yet the 'house', although requiring close co-operation, was not a joint-tenancy, nor did its inhabitants constitute a kinship group. The farm was not communal, but the very reverse. Run-rig achieved a precise definition of each tenant's entitlement as an individual. A clear understanding of these entitlements was the best guarantee of the 'good neighbourhood' which living and working in close proximity required.

In theory each 'house' within the township should also have received its proportionate share according to its merks in the same way as land within a 'house' was shared by tenants. However, there was nothing like the same precision. When Laxobigging's 'houses' are compared, wide variations are found, no doubt because there were seldom adjustments between 'houses', although re-allocations within the 'house' were frequent, being required whenever there was a change in the number of tenants. Hence, the 'house' of Sugarder had 0.95 acres of arable for each merk, whereas Toftins with 0.45 acres had less than half that amount. Similarly the proportion of land which was infield varied from 83% in Millburn to only 18% in Sugarder.

In terms of ownership and tenancy, the farm of Laxo (fig 49) was very like Graven; this 17 merk farm also had two owners and three tenants. However, it did not form a consolidated block as at Graven. A good deal of its arable land did cluster around the house sites, but there were many outlying rigs scattered throughout the three-quarter mile length of the township lying intermingled with the farms of Niegarth, Sugarder and Toftins. Thus Laxo exhibited a further degree of run-rig where the 'house' itself was dispersed. The three tenants again lived in close proximity, with even the farm-yard portioned off into an incredible ten run-rig sections, and they made hay "in company". However, the dispersed nature of the farm resulted in their arable land lying run-rig, not just with each other, but also with tenants of other farms, and most of the grassland was held in common, not only among the two proprietors and three tenants of Laxo, but also with the people from the neighbouring farms of Toftins and Niegarth. In these circumstances the concept of the 'house', although still important, was somewhat weaker than at Graven.

Even in 1827 the smaller Laxobigging 'houses' of Niegarth (4 acres), Sugarder (3.8 acres), Hoya (4.2 acres), Millburn (1.6 acres) and Sandibanks (3.9 acres) were still single tenancies, although their lands were all to a greater or lesser extent run-rig with other farms. Given that the population of Delting had more than doubled, and that landlords had been actively creating new holdings, it is possible to envisage a period prior to the middle of the eighteenth century when a single tenant had more often than not held the bigger farms of Toftins (6.8 acres), Laxo (10.2 acres) and Graven (12.8 acres). The 'house' was regarded as a theoretical family farm, although custom dictated that it might from time to time be subdivided, a practice no doubt encouraged in the past by udal division between co-heirs. Formerly there had usually been less inter-mixture of the 'houses' and much less run-rig, although a certain amount of farm division had always been a feature of Shetland land-holding. On 14 February 1576/7 Thomas of Laxvo and Magnus of

112

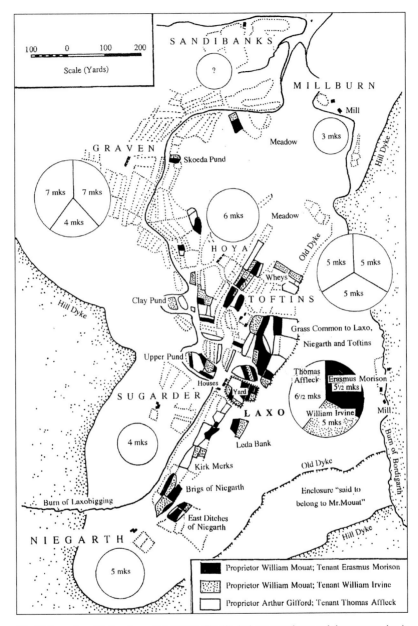

Fig 49. Laxo, Laxobigging. Laxo, like Graven (Fig 48), had two proprietors and three tenants, but it represents a further degree of run-rig, since it was less compact. Its arable land was often run-rig with other farms. Note how Laxo had spread southwards into Niegarth's territory, as shown by places with... *of Niegarth*-names. Pie-charts show tenant-holdings within each 'house'.

113

Laxvo were sworn to be examined; they were two heads of households sharing the farm of Laxo[10].

Before turning to the question of the disappearance of Shetland 'house', it is worth noting that the 'house' was an ancient institution of a type at one time common throughout Western Europe, being related to land units widely found in Germanic, Scandinavian, Celtic and former Roman areas[11]. When we read about a villa in Carolingian France divided into 12 manses, and the 12 manses occupied by 32 households, we readily recognise the same three levels of organisation as township, 'house' and tenant-holding[12]. The Latin term *mansus* was translated into English as 'hide', and the hide was originally equated with a notional household — Bede's *"terra unius familiae"* (land of one family) — but, in the same way as a Shetland 'house' often comprised more than one household, the hide or manse might in practice be shared by more than one real family. Even before 1000 AD the land of these multi-tenanted notional family units was often dispersed, yet the manse or hide remained the unit within which the *socii* (partners) were left to sort out their obligations of rent and services. Like the Shetland 'house', it was the unit within which sharing took place, and the interface between ordinary folk and their masters. Hides were used as fiscal units and deemed to be equal, and so there was a need to impose a definition upon them which, in the arable English landscape, was done in terms of area. Area was a less satisfactory definition where arable land was discontinuous, as in Shetland, and it was easier to work with equal value units. In Shetland the 'house' often came to be equated with the 'last' of land, the unit which paid 144 'pennies' in rent. Brian Smith has described the usefulness of the last for township layout. Lasts were a series of large equal-value 'boxes' within which shares could be determined and the land could be laid out in run-rig[13].

By the eleventh and twelfth century, manses in France became so fragmented that they gradually vanished, with each separate portion becoming saddled with its own responsibilities for rent and services, and these changes also affected England and Germany a century later. It was only in the second half of the eighteenth century, however that the Shetland 'houses' disappeared, their decay being brought about by the same process of fragmentation and dispersal resulting from an increasing population. Thus Laxobigging, which was unusual in that its 'houses' were still functional as late as 1827, exhibits features which disappeared from more central parts of Europe six or seven hundred years earlier.

William Balfour who acted as chamberlain of the Dundas estate in Shetland from 1769 to 1778 was puzzled by Shetland's vanishing 'houses'; in fact, not being a Shetlander, he was puzzled by the very concept of the 'house'. In his Rental of the Lordship of Shetland (1772) he remarked that Gott was properly speaking a "house" rather than a township, because its lands lay run-rig with Veensgarth and Uresland, and were so inter-mixed that they could not be distinguished except by the inhabitants. Yet he noted that:

> ... the possessors of Uresland and Vinsgarth occupy not their proportions of the land of Goat, nor those of Goat their proportions of the towns of Uresland and Vinsgarth, which can only be accounted for by supposing that the antient inhabitants exchanged land with each other[14].

He was describing dispersed 'houses' not unlike Laxo, but much bigger, lying intermixed, yet with a good deal of their land in the vicinity of the house sites. Since the land was run-rig, Balfour imagined that the holdings of the Gott tenants had originally been dispersed in a regular fashion throughout the combined Gott-Veensgarth-Uresland township; he envisaged that the land had become concentrated around the 'house' sites as a result of informal exchanges made for the sake of convenience, and he may have known instances of this kind of unofficial consolidation from his native Orkney[15]. In reality precisely the opposite was happening; the one-time relatively self-contained farms were beginning to break up and to merge. Balfour remarked that the lands next to Gott were "exceeding mean"; he considered that "ten or twelve farm houses crowded close as they can stand hath contributed not a little to render the lands of Goat such as they are"[16]. However, he failed to make the further connection between the over-population and squalor of the tightly nucleated "Gott Closs"[17] and the fact that its land was merging with neighbouring 'houses' in complicated patterns of run-rig.

Balfour's commentary on his rental shows us that there were many other places where the 'house' structure was disappearing as early as 1772. At Houbie in Fetlar he noted that the township had formerly consisted of five distinct 'houses'. At Gruting, in the same island, 'houses' which existed in name only caused problems since 'kingsland', for which he was responsible, was properly in certain 'houses' rather than in the township as a whole[18]. At Clibberswick in Unst he commented that "the lands all ly run-rig in one and the same town, tho' under different names or designations". He also visited the adjoining township of Norwick, where he noted that:

Digron, Turvhoul [Troll], Kirkatoun and Sandeal in Norwick are the names not of separate towns but of houses in one town consisting of 128 merks land[19], all lying run-rig together[20].

Farms "all lying run-rig together" takes us a stage beyond the partial intermixture which was found at Laxobigging and Gott. A detailed survey of Norwick made in 1822 by Thomas Irvine allows us to see more clearly the pattern which Balfour was trying to describe.

Norwick (fig 50) was a fishing station and so was more directly affected than Laxobigging by the development of commercial fishing. As was often the case in large Shetland townships, landownership patterns were exceedingly complex, with no less than nine proprietors, of whom only the minister and one proprietor were resident. One of the absentees lived in Yell and owned a mere half-merk[21], approximately a 1/280th share of the township. We do not know the number of tenant-holdings in 1822 in the 'houses' of Digron, Sandale, Kirkatoun and Troll (Virse was the minister's glebe), but by mid-century Norwick had no less than 208 inhabitants in 38 households. Digron, Sandale and Kirkatoun were all closely grouped on the north side of a prominent mound on which stood the remains of the Chapel of St. John. Since each of these 'houses' consisted of several households,

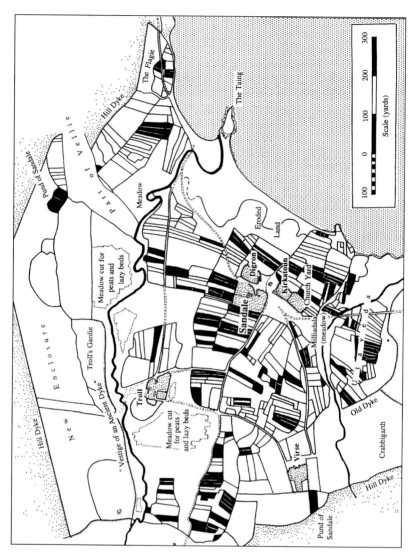

Fig 50. Sandale, Norwick. The 'house' of Sandale existed in little more than name, its arable land being dispersed in 128 parcels throughout this very extensive town ship. Thomas Irvine's survey, despite its attention to detail, was not very accurate, exaggerating east-west relative to north-south dimensions.

and since the 'houses' themselves were closely grouped, the result was a single multi-house nucleated settlement.

In the latter part of the eighteenth century the land on the seaward side of the township was badly affected by sand-blow, perhaps as the result of the combined effects of more intensive cultivation and the depredations of pigs. Thomas Irvine was of the opinion that "the swine has done more damage to Norwick than all the other agents of destruction together"[22]. Erosion was unchecked, although Balfour noted that it might have been easily halted had it been tackled in time[23]. In 1822 the surveyor described how the outline of former rigs disappeared under the sand[24], and for a time there was talk that the houses in the very nucleus of the settlement might have to be removed[25]. Understandably, no one would willingly agree to have the bulk of his land in this part of the township, yet proprietors were torn in two directions since everyone was determined to retain access to the shore because of the fishing interests, and also for the seaweed on which the manuring of the land depended. These contrary considerations were important factors in the development of the very dispersed pattern of the Norwick farms.

At Laxobigging each 'house' had its own general location within the township, and even at Laxo, the least cohesive of its farms, much of the land still tended to be concentrated around the house sites. However, at Norwick as the 1822 surveyor remarked, "names apply only to certain houses or steadings; there are no particular boundaries making separate rooms"[26]; the land of each 'house' lay in what may be described as 'whole-township run-rig', scattered throughout the length and breadth of the township (fig 50). Yet, despite its spread, the distribution was neither regular, nor was it altogether random. The 'houses' were mostly held by two or more owners, each typically having several tenants, and so rigs were often laid off in adjacent pairs or in groups, apparently for purposes of easy comparison. Once again we see the principle that it was equality within the farm which was the important consideration. Farms also came into the reckoning for minor purposes such as the ownership of certain 'punds' (enclosures) which lay on the margins of the township, some of which can be dated as post-1720 intakes. These punds pertained to 'houses', rather than to individual tenants and proprietors, and so complicated fractions of proprietorial and tenant run-rig were transferred outwards on to new land. For example the tiny pund of Sandale Be-East, which stood high on the rim of the township and was only one-third of an acre in extent, required to be shared proportionally; thus William Mouat of Garth, part owner of Sandale, was entitled to 3/8 of it. For most practical purposes however, the 'house' structure had disappeared.

This concept of 'whole township run-rig' was carried to its ultimate conclusion at Funzie. Farms at Laxobigging were still working units, at Norwick some vestigial functions remained, but in Funzie the very concept of the 'house' had disappeared as far as the management of land was concerned. Funzie had nine tenants who rented 7 merks each and lived on terms of strict equality, although they were not all tenants of the same laird. Throughout the entire township rigs were counted off in groups of nine, one rig being allocated to each tenant (fig 51). Within each group the tenants' rigs did not appear in any regular order, so it is likely that they had been allocated by lot. Grassland was similarly divided into a multitude of little grazing sections and allocated in the same way. The net result was the maximum possible dispersal of each tenant's land in 'whole township run-rig' throughout what was again a very large township. These changes were accompanied by the abandonment of several of the peripherally-situated house-sites, and the concentration of settlement in the middle of the township, possibly because of the advantages of the central location when land is dispersed in a regular pattern. William Henderson of Thoft had an average journey of 250 yards to reach his infield rigs but, had he lived at the outlying (and abandoned) house at Siggataft, his average journey would have been about 600 yards — more than twice as much. Minimising distance must have been an important consideration in the absence of carts when manure needed to be transported to maintain rigs in infield cultivation[27].

We happen to know that Funzie had possessed a farm structure in 1616[28], and these self-contained farms, perhaps not unlike those of Laxobigging, were still in existence in 1776. In that year Thomas Sanderson of Buness wrote to Sir John Mitchell of Westshore suggesting that it would be to their mutual advantage to divide the 'room' of Nurgie[29]. Nurgie was one of the Funzie 'houses' and had 9 merks of land, 2 merks being in the possession of a Mr Sinclair who was Sanderson's tenant, and the remaining 7 merks being farmed by James Smith who was Sir John Mitchell's factor. The two tenants farmed in run-rig, but Sanderson proposed that their lands should be separated, with each given his due proportion of corn grounds, grass and meadow. Sanderson obviously thought that this division would be a simple matter (it appears that it could be done without affecting the other people in Funzie) so it is clear that in 1776 Nurgie was still a reasonably compact two-tenant farm.

Three years earlier (1773) William Balfour had tried to abolish run-rig throughout Funzie, and the township had been measured under his direction, but the attempt collapsed when a small proprietor refused to agree[30]. However, instead of doing away with run-rig, which seemed to be most people's intention in the 1770s provided they could avoid legal expenses, Funzie was subjected to further degrees of fragmentation and dispersal. At an unknown date between 1776 and 1829 its whole structure was radically altered, its 'houses' were abolished, to be replaced by the very regular whole-township run-rig pattern which we find in the 1829 survey. The fact that neither the proposed nor the actual changes seem to have involved recourse to the Sheriff Court and official procedures, should make us wary of making statements about the frequency of re-organisation on the basis of legal records. Sanderson's proposed division of Nurgie illustrates the ease with which reallocation could be achieved as long as a township retained its 'house' structure. Agreement between two proprietors, as at Nurgie, might often be achieved on an informal basis. Where there was a single owner, as was often the case with smaller 'houses', re-allocation to tenants was even easier, requiring no formalities, and no doubt it was a very frequent occurrence. Once the stage of whole-township run-rig was reached, informal re-allocations were not so easy. In contrast to earlier informal agreements, the attempted division of Funzie in 1829 was taken to the

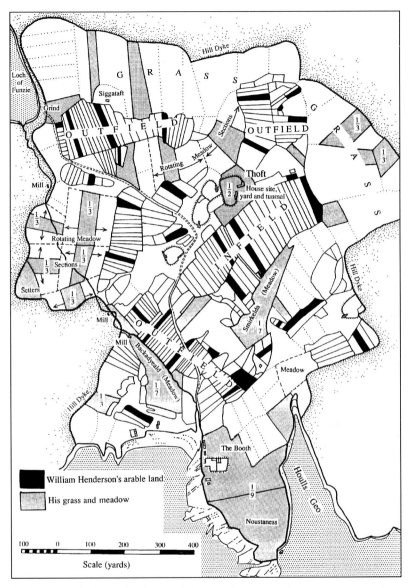

Fig 51. William Henderson's Holding, Funzie. In Funzie the 'house' structure disappeared prior to 1829, the tenants' holdings being distributed in whole-township run-rig. Arrows indicate rotating meadow-sections each worked by teams of three tenants. Fractions indicate 'halvers' sections, shared by groups of tenants, or sometimes by all nine tenants in common. Compare the increasing degrees of farm dispersal shown in Figs 47 to 51.

119

Sheriff Court, where the whole process eventually collapsed amid acrimonious and expensive disputes.

Whole-township run-rig, which involved the disappearance of the 'house' structure, also involved the abandonment of systems of internal divisions such as garths, punds and inner dykes. Enclosures decayed, and a more open landscape developed. We have already noted the existence of punds at Norwick but it is at Laxobigging that punds can be seen most clearly (fig 52). The township had ten punds, mainly located along the Burn of Laxobigging and varying in size from about 0.3 to 2.0 acres, while further *whey*-names (O.N. *kvi*, enclosure) indicate the former existence of more features of the same type.

Names such as 'the Pund of Graven' and 'Niegard's Pund' show that these punds had in the not-so-distant past been attached as whole units to the 'houses' of Graven and Niegarth, although Niegard's Pund was at the other end of the township, three-quarters of a mile away from its parent farm. Punds had been primarily enclosures where animals were impounded, although the accumulation of manure allowed intermittent cultivation. In eighteenth century Skye, little stock enclosures with "ubiquitous turf dykes" were a common feature of the crofting landscape[31], and the Laxobigging punds must at one time have presented a similar appearance. By 1827 they were punds in name only. All trace of surrounding dykes had disappeared, the connection with individual farms had been severed, and the former punds had, without exception, been thrown into the general pool of run-rig arable land.

Quite a different type of enclosure was associated with garth-names (O.N. *garðr*, an enclosure). Garths were much bigger than punds and consisted of large tracts of rough grassland running out to the hill dyke (fig 53). Some garths developed into independent 'houses' with a marginal location, as at Sugarder and Niegarth (Laxobigging) and Gardie and Siggataft (Funzie), but the land was mostly incapable of being brought into cultivation. At Laxobigging the garths were described by the surveyor as "deep and mossy", "wet and broken", and as "swamp". Indeed most of this land was, and still is, indistinguishable from unimproved hill grazing. Two of these Laxobigging intakes were recent[32], but the main garth-creating phase can probably be dated to a period well back into the Middle Ages. The garth-names, the Gardens of Hoya, Sugarder and Niegarth, illustrate a sequence of development as Laxobigging pushed southwards by enclosing areas of hill land. The first and oldest of these garths is the Gardens of Hoya ('gardens' = plural of 'garth'); Sugarder, 'the south garth' is 'south' in relation to the Gardens, but it was only 'south' until Niegarth, the 'new garth' came into existence even farther south. Yet by 1577 Niegarth existed, not just as an enclosure, but as a farm, since Olaw of Neagarth was one of the inhabitants of Delting sworn to give evidence regarding Earl Robert Stewart's oppressions[33]. It follows that all three garths must be older than 1577, perhaps much older.

Early information on agricultural practices which may have relevance to the process of garth-creation is contained in the 1298 Faroese *Sheep Letter* which permitted the continuation of certain local customs despite the reform of Gulathing

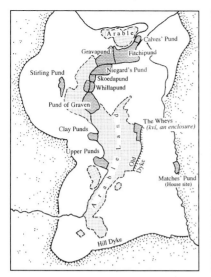

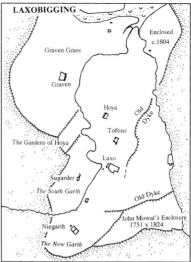

Fig 52. Laxobigging Punds. These punds had originally been little turf-walled stock enclosures. Further 'whey-names' indicate more features of the same type. Some names show that punds in the not-so-distant past had been attached to specific 'houses', but by 1827 this connection had been severed and they had all been brought into cultivation as part of the general pool of run-rig arable land.

Fig 53. Garths at Laxobigging. Garths were tracts of poor quality grassland running out to the hill dyke. The intakes in the south and north-east date from the late eighteenth and early nineteenth century, but the sequence of garths to the west (the Gardens of Hoya, Sugarder and Niegarth) are medieval grazing enclosures.

Fig 54. Garths at Funzie. Prominent inner dykes beyond which garth-names are to be found indicate the existence of former grazing enclosures. By 1829 these garths had been abandoned, and the land was laid off in numerous small sections of run-rig grass on which animals required to be tethered.

121

law, and there is reason to believe that these regulations may have covered Shetland as well as Faroe. The letter suggests important distinctions between 'wild' sheep which pastured together on the scattald, and 'tame' sheep which were kept on individually-owned grassland adjacent to the home fields, that is in garths[34]. Since wadmel (woollen cloth) was one of the principal commodities in which Shetland tax was paid, it is not surprising to find that the medieval landscape included systems of enclosures connected with sheep husbandry.

A similar series of garths was to be found at Funzie (fig 54) where the remains of an ancient-looking inner dyke of very large up-ended stones is still a prominent feature. As at Laxobigging, a series of garths, Turrigard, Gardie, and two Lingagards, lay outside the old dyke, while Whilvapund, although not a garth-name, was a similar enclosure. The old dyke, apparently a hill dyke beyond which the township had expanded when the garths were created, was preserved because of its usefulness as an inner dyke, protecting the cultivated land from stock within the garths, but by 1829 the divisions between one garth and the next had been abandoned, and the inner dyke was ruinous.

Ruinous inner dykes which had once separated garths from the arable land were to be found at Laxobigging (figs 49 and 53) and Norwick (fig 50) as well as at Funzie, and indeed the frequency with which internal dykes are mentioned suggests that they were a standard feature of most townships. At Clibberswick, which bounds Norwick to the south, a mid-nineteenth century map shows the remains of internal dykes beyond which lay the garth-names, Evragardie and Valdsgarth[35], while at Baliasta, also in Unst, the garth-named farms of Hundagarth and Gerragarth were similarly separated from the rest of the township by "vestages of old dykes"[36]. Early sixteenth century Court Books provide evidence that dykes were fully operational at that date. In Earl Patrick's time William Sinclair of Ustaness was "ordanit with his nychbouris to put upe [i.e. repair] the inner dykis" in order that the complainer might be safe from damage done by animals. Similarly Erasmus in Framgord, Unst, was ordered to keep a lawful pund so that the corn and grass of the tenants of Maill and Colvidale should be safe from his sheep, and a heavy £10 fine was imposed on him two years later because he had failed to comply. There were also complains about "unlawful dykes" at Still (Fetlar), and Pettafirth (Bressay), presumably because these dykes created garths, or otherwise took into individual tenure, land to which other people had rights[37].

The maintenance of dykes which, if built of turf, required annual repair was always a problem. The inclusion within Laxobigging of large poor-quality garths was of very doubtful benefit, given the length of dyke which was needed to enclose them. The fourteen tenants had a township perimeter of over three miles to keep up, besides considerable lengths of inner dykes and punds. In many places the remains of Laxobigging's hill dyke cannot nowadays be located, suggesting that even the outer dyke was never a very substantial structure. Although the township continued to expand outwards[38], the internal dykes enclosing garths were abandoned in favour of the practice of tethering the animals. Possibly this change occurred when increasing population made it no longer possible to allocate garths as whole units. If garths needed to be shared, and sharing required animals to be tethered, the function of the enclosure was lost and there was little point in keeping up internal dykes.

At Funzie the abandonment of the garths resulted in most of the grass being laid out in run-rig, with no less than 92 individual grazing lots. The corners of these plots are likely to have been marked by stones or else by little pits known as 'boot holes'[39] (O.N. *beita*, to use for pasture), exactly comparable to the 'station-holes' of Irish rundale. Poorer grass sections were shared by groups of tenants ("halvers' grass"), and the exposed headland of Noustaness was held by all nine tenants in common, as was the outlying section known as Setters (possibly a milking place).

The changes which were taking place in Shetland run-rig find close parallels in Irish rundale which had the same three organisational levels of township, farm and tenant-holding, and where 'farms' were disappearing into whole-township run-rig just like the Shetland 'houses'[40]. The result was a landscape of incredible complexity. One Irishman, a tailor to trade, described to the Devon Commission how he had finally given up his land in despair because it lay in 42 different places, with the result that "it would take a very keen man to find it"[41]. By that standard, there must have been many 'keen' Shetlanders. Funzie was 183 acres, but was divided into close on 500 run-rig parcels. The Irishman might complain about his 42 portions, but in Funzie William Henderson's land lay in no less than 61 distinct sections (fig 51). William Henderson was primarily a fisherman, but he had a shared yard, 9 infield and 23 outfield rigs, 9 shared meadow sections, and 19 widely scattered grazing sections delineated by markers which he might or might not be able to locate. Some grazing sections were little more than a spot on which a cow might be tethered (and there were sharp-eyed neighbours on the look-out for an over-long tether). Understandably Shetlanders were sometimes in the same predicament as the Devon Commission's bewildered Irishman. When Thomas Irvine surveyed Norwick in 1822, he reported that "the tenants were in many instances ignorant of the marches of their slips of meadow and grass"[42]. The complexity needed to achieve equality eventually overtook the ability of the tenants to comprehend it.

I have so far avoided the question 'Why?'. To the modern mind it is difficult to understand why people chose to lay out land in what seems to have been a thoroughly inconvenient way. However, it is worth noting that run-rig was not a system imposed on reluctant tenants by their landlords. The people trying to abolish run-rig were always lairds, ministers, surveyors, estate factors and agricultural theorists, in short, 'the people above'. William Balfour was an early critic of the system, and his views are typical; he condemned run-rig at Funzie, commenting that "it holds universally the more extensive the town and the more farmers upon it, the poorer they are"; splitting possessions and multiplying families had been "a great error" and the people, who had once been "bold and expert fishermen", were now "dispirited, poor, negligent and unenterprising". It was by abolishing run-rig and "laying a man's farm adjacent to his house and midding dung that the land is to be improved in this country"[43].

The people who had devised the run-rig landscape, and wished to retain it, were the tenants themselves. Despite all the efforts which Matthewson expended on surveying Funzie and producing his marvellous map, the proposed abolition of run-rig came to nothing. As late as 1833 Matthewson offered to undertake a completely new division according to a different scheme, although he predicted that this would not be popular with the tenants:

> The Funzie men want the whole [township] run-rig so as to have equal share of everything because they have equal rents. They are particularly desirous of having it runrig at least this year. But I find on considering the subject that these reasons will for ever be the same and having seen nothing but the runrig plan they know little of any other[44].

To "have equal shares of everything because they have equal rents" or, more precisely, to have shares strictly proportional to merks in terms both of quantity and quality, was the very key to understanding run-rig. Sharing all the resources available to the community according to an individual's entitlement was a very ancient principle, firmly embedded in the Shetland consciousness, and as old as the concept of the scattald[45]. The preservation of 'good neighbourhood' was a vital consideration, and it depended on the sharing being done in a way which everyone recognised as fair. In the final analysis fairness was more important than convenience.

In a landscape where resources of arable land, meadow and grass were scarce and were unevenly distributed, a certain amount of run-rig was endemic. What caused it to flourish to such an absurd extent in the eighteenth and early nineteenth centuries was partly pressure of population and the desire of lairds to accommodate more fishing tenants. However, run-rig also reflected a certain kind of society: one where small farms were crowded together, but without any person, rural court, or other mechanism, whereby decisions could be taken and solutions imposed. What the tenant received from the landlord was an entitlement to a share. William Balfour's admission that the complex run-rig at Veensgarth, Uresland and Gott "could not be distinguished except by the inhabitants" illustrates the extent to which the process whereby tenants translated shares into actual land was largely incomprehensible to the owners of the land. Landlords of dispersed Shetland estates had other economic interests, they hardly understood, or wished to understand, the complexities of the agricultural landscape, and they always hoped that matters might be settled with a minimum of trouble and expense. In these circumstances run-rig was the tenants' preferred solution; perhaps it was the only solution.

It is not my intention to examine in any detail the wider significance of the changes which have been identified. Similarities in topography, social structure and demographic pressure created many close parallels between Shetland run-rig and the rundale system in Ireland, and the same kind of links with Scottish practice can readily be found. However, it would be worth investigating whether the processes which affected Shetland in the eighteenth and early nineteenth century have a wider application in quite different environmental conditions, such as in the development of dispersed open-field systems in the arable districts of England in the early medieval period. In Shetland, and perhaps also in areas where 'open-field' developed, a sequence of changes was set in motion by a rapid increase in population which caused the intermediate level of organisation based on the notional single-family unit (the 'house', manse or hide) to become increasingly fragmented with the result that it ceased to function for agricultural purposes. This brought about a shift to whole-township organisation which in turn produced a much increased degree of dispersal. As long as the 'house' was operational, informal redistribution of individual entitlements was easy but, with its disappearance, re-allocation became difficult, and dispersed patterns tended to become frozen, as in England. Dispersal also encouraged the development of centrally-located settlements which in Shetland were sometimes tightly nucleated although, in terms of numbers, they fell far short of the populous English agricultural villages. At the same time the abandonment of internal dykes and enclosures resulted in a landscape which, although more limited in scale, might also be described as an 'open-field' system.

Acknowledgements

My thanks are due to Brian Smith, Shetland Archivist, with whom I have discussed run-rig over a period of many years; he brought to my notice many of the documents used in this paper. I am also grateful to George Sutherland, Lerwick, and to John and Wendy Scott, Bressay, for permission to make use of the maps of Laxobigging and Norwick which are respectively in their possession.

References

1   William P.L. Thomson, 'Funzie, Fetlar; a Shetland Run-Rig Township in the Nineteenth Century', *Scottish Geographical Magazine*, Vol. 86, No. 3, 1970.

2   Desmond McCourt, *'The Rundale System in Ireland; a Study in its Geographical Distribution and Social Relations'*, unpublished Ph.D thesis, Queen's University, Belfast, 1950; Desmond McCourt, 'The Dynamic Quality of Irish Rural Settlement', in Emrys Innes and Desmond McCourt (eds.), *Man and his Habitat*, 1971.

3   Desmond McCourt, *'The Rundale System in Ireland'*, p. 43.

4   D.J. Withrington and I.R. Grant (eds.), *The Statistical Account of Scotland*, Vol. xix (cited as *OSA* = Old Statistical Account), Parish of Delting, p. 411.

5   *OSA*, Parish of Delting, p. 407.

6   In 1773 the arable land at Funzie was estimated to be 60 acres of which 32% was infield. By 1829 the cultivated area was probably unchanged, although now measured as 58 acres, but the proportion of infield had increased to 45%. However, 'infield' and 'outfield' were Scottish terms, rather than indigenous to Shetland run-rig. Instead of an infield-outfield 'system', individual rigs were cultivated with varying degrees of frequency, and the description of them as 'infield' and 'outfield' was sometimes a matter of individual judgement.

7   *OSA*, Parish of Delting, p. 410.

8   Funzie (surveyor, A.D. Matthewson), Shetland Archives, SC.12/6/1828/48 and SC.12/6/1829/3; Laxobigging (surveyor, A.D. Matthewson), in possession of George Sutherland, Lerwick; Norwick (surveyor, Thomas Irvine), in possession of John and Wendy Scott, Gardie House, Bressay.

9   There was some confusion about the total merks in Laxobigging, probably caused by uncertainty whether some of its merks ought to be assigned to 'outsets' (new settlement). In 1827 Laxobigging was sometimes regarded as 68 merks and at other times as 71 merks. It seems likely that the total had originally been 72 merks. Hoya's merks also varied, being recorded as 11¼merks in 1631, but only 6 merks in 1827.

10 David Balfour, *Oppressions of the Sixteenth Century in the Islands of Orkney and Shetland*, 1859, p. 27.

11 F.W. Maitland, *The Domesday Book and Beyond*, (1897), 1960, pp. 416-421, 591-594; T.M. Charles-Edwards, 'Kinship, Status and the Origin of the Hide', *Past and Present*, No. 56, 1972.

12 Marc Bloch, *French Rural History*, 1966, p.160 (*Les Caractères Originaux de l'Histoire Rurale Francaise*, Oslo and Paris, 1931).

13 Brian Smith, *Rentals of the Lordship of Shetland, c. 1500-1716,* Forthcoming.

14 William Balfour, mss.*Rental of the Lordship of Shetland*, Orkney Archives, D2/2.

15 J. Storer Clouston, 'The Orkney Townships', *Scottish Historical Review*, Vol. 17, 1919, p.29.

16 William Balfour, Rental of the Lordship of Shetland.

17 The late George Nelson told John Graham that he had heard his grandfather use this name for the pre-Clearance settlement.

18 William Balfour, *Rental of the Lordship of Shetland*, p. 62.

19 At the time of the 1822 survey Norwick was regarded as containing 140 merks.

20 William Balfour, *Rental of the Lordship of Shetland*, p. 56.

21 Complaint by the Rt. Hon. Thomas Dundas craving division, 27 June 1817. Shetland Archives, SC.12/6/6115, box xxvii.

22 Thomas Irvine, mss. *Report on the Survey of Norwick*, No. IV.

23 William Balfour, *Rental of the Lordship of Shetland*, p. 56.

24 Thomas Irvine, *Report on the Survey of Norwick*, No. IV.

25 William Balfour, *Rental of the Lordship of Shetland*, p. 56.

26 Thomas Irvine, *Report upon the survey of Norwick*, No. IV.

27 At Norwick, Thomas Irvine noted that it was not so much the quality of the land as distance from farmyard manure and seaweed which determined whether land was cultivated as infield or outfield.

28 Steelbow agreement between the Rev. Patrik Hog, minister of Fetlar, and Johne Archear, now dwelling in Garth, Fetlar, Scottish Record Office, Register of Commisariot Deeds of Orkney and Shetland, Vol. 1, folios 50-1. "Garth" is Gardie.

29 Letter, Thomas Sanderson of Buness to Sir John Mitchell of Westshore, 22 July 1776, Shetland Archives SC.12/53/6.

30 William Balfour, *Rental of the Lordship of Shetland*.

31 Malcolm D. MacSween, 'Transhumance in North Skye', *Scottish Geographical Magazine*, Vol. 75, No. 2, 1959; Robert A. Dodgshon, 'Medieval Rural Scotland', in G. Whittington and I.D. Whyte, *An Historical Geography of Scotland*, 1983, p. 65.

32 The enclosure east of the Burn of Bordigarth was the subject of a dispute which reached the Sheriff Court, where it transpired that the enclosure was created c. 1804. The other enclosure beyond the old dyke in the south of the township dated from the time of John Mouat of Garth, b. 1751 d. 1824.

33 David Balfour, *Oppressions of the Sixteenth Century in the Islands of Orkney and Shetland*, 1859, p.27.

34 *Seyðabraeviô*, Tórshavn, 1971; G.V.C. Young, *From the Vikings to the Reformation; a Chronicle of the Faroe Islands up to 1538*, 1979, pp. 140-153.

35　Division of Clibberswick, 1842-47, Shetland Archives, SC.12/6/1842/167.

36　Division of Baliasta, 1797-1801, Shetland Archives, SC.12/6/1305/Box xv.

37　Gordon Donaldson, *Shetland Life under Earl Patrick*, 1958, pp. 39-40.

38　See note 32.

39　Alexander Fenton, 'The Traditional Pastoral Economy', in M.L. Parry and T.R. Slater, *The Making of the Scottish Countryside*, 1980.

40　As well as Desmond McCourt's work cited in Note 2, see Ronald H. Buchanan, 'Field Systems of Ireland', in A.R.H. Baker and R.A. Butlin, *Studies of Field Systems of the British Isles*, 1973.

41　Desmond McDourt, *'The Rundale System in Ireland'*, p. 37, quoting the Devon Commission, Vol. 3, p. 798.

42　Thomas Irvine, *Report upon the Survey of Norwick*, No. IV, Shetland Archives, SC.12/6/6115.

43　William Balfour, *Rental of the Lordship of Shetland*, pp. 64 and 82.

44　Mss. letter, Andrew D. Matthewson, 24 January 1833, Shetland Archives, D.23/42.

45　Brian Smith, 'What is a Scattald?', in Barbara E. Crawford, *Essays in Shetland History*, 1984.

INTERPRETING THE SOIL LANDSCAPE OF PAPA STOUR

Stephen Carter & Donald Davidson

The Soil Landscape of Papa Stour

Anyone who has visited the island of Papa Stour and walked from the pier, westwards across the island, is struck by the contrast between the green, fertile agricultural land of the eastern half and the brown, stony hill land of the western half of the island. The dividing line between the two halves is the old hill dyke, now redundant but still standing, and this points to the cause of the great contrast. The soil from the former common grazings in the west of the island has quite literally been carried, as turves, into the old arable land within the dyke. Here it was used as fuel for the hearth and in the byre as bedding but ultimately it was all spread on the fields to fertilise the crops. As the turf stripping progressed, the hill land became increasingly stony and bare and the soils of the cultivated rigs became deeper and deeper.

A declining population, and changes in agricultural methods mean that turf is now hardly used in the island. Turf dykes have been replaced by post and wire fences; coal or peat from the mainland is now used for fuel; no one needs turves for their roof thatching or byre bedding and other fertilisers are available for what little arable cropping occurs in the island. As a result, over the last fifty years or thereabouts, the soil on the hill has begun to re-form and the vegetation recover. It is testimony to the past severity of the process that the striking contrast remains today, long after scalping ceased. The present-day soil landscape of Papa Stour is therefore a persistent legacy of traditional land-use practices that have now all but disappeared.

Turf Manuring and the Study of Ancient Agriculture

The use of turf as a fertiliser of cultivated soils was by no means limited to Papa Stour; indeed variations of it occurred throughout Scotland and similar practices are recorded from Ireland and continental north-west Europe where the deepened cultivation soils are referred to as *plaggen* soils (from the German word meaning a turf). The origins of plaggen soils and turf manuring remain unclear but recent studies in Scotland point to the use of closely related agricultural techniques as early as the Bronze Age (Dockrill *et al* 1994).

The authors' interest in Papa Stour developed from their studies of the impact of ancient agricultural practice on soils and the landscape. It is difficult to understand prehistoric agriculture with only the evidence of the soil to work from and one solution to this problem is to study the soils from present-day examples of traditional agricultural systems. In this way changes in the soils can be clearly linked to the particular agricultural practices that caused them. The final years of the traditional agricultural system in Papa Stour were recorded by Alexander Fenton in one of his pioneering studies in Scottish Ethnography. His accounts, combined with the information available from other documentary sources and local people who witnessed some of the old ways of land-management, offered the opportunity to study the impact of a well-recorded traditional agricultural system on the landscape. In common with all small islands, Papa Stour had the added advantage of offering a self-contained system of manageable size, ideal for such a study.

Our research has involved two main tasks. Firstly, we have used the documentary records to reconstruct the traditional agricultural system of the island, focusing on cultivation practice and the use of turf. Then, secondly, we have studied the cultivated soils themselves to discover what the effects of the cultivation have been. By combining the results of documentary and soils research we can discover those aspects of the traditional system that leave any traces in the soil and those that have no apparent impact. The conclusions will be applied in archaeological studies, leading we hope, to a better understanding of prehistoric agriculture.

Traditional Agriculture in Papa Stour

The starting point of our research was Fenton's account of the traditional agricultural methods of the island which is published primarily in his book 'The Northern Isles: Orkney and Shetland' (Fenton 1978). What he described was an agricultural landscape, formerly common throughout Shetland, consisting of cultivated land and pasture divided from extensive common grazings by an enclosing dyke. In Papa Stour almost all of the settlement was within the one dyke with only the two outsets of Hamnavoe and North Banks forming discrete holdings outside of that dyke. The cultivated land was formerly organised into numerous rigs, small strips and blocks of land, with the holdings of the various tenants intermixed. The soil was cultivated with the delling spade and the crops of barley, oats and potatoes were fertilised with a variety of materials including turf, byre muck and seaweed. The livestock that produced the muck were stalled at night in the byre; they grazed in summer on the hill and, after the harvest, within the town dyke. Turf was cut, by right, in the common grazings and used in a variety of ways: to make dykes, on house roofs, as a fuel, in the byre as bedding or as a component of muck heaps. In all cases it ended up on the field because none of this valuable resource was wasted as dykes were demolished, houses re-roofed or ashes cleaned from the hearth.

For the purposes of our study, it was important to establish the history of the agricultural practices recorded by Fenton in the mid-twentieth century. Soils evolve over long periods of time and therefore could have been influenced by radically different land-use practices in the past. There are few documents that are relevant to the history of agriculture in the island but those which exist have already been studied, principally by Alexander Fenton, Brian Smith (Shetland Archivist) and Barbara Crawford (University of St. Andrews) (see Smith 1985, Crawford 1984). The following account draws heavily on their conclusions.

The Historical Development of Agriculture in Papa Stour

Prehistoric and Medieval Origins

From the work of Smith and Crawford, it is clear that the present day two-fold division of the island was established by the later Norse period (roughly AD 1300) when documentary, place-name and archaeological evidence demonstrate that settlement was limited to the eastern half of the island. Settlement in earlier periods was more widespread and today there are the remains of early prehistoric houses and burnt mounds out in what is now the denuded hill land as well as within the town dyke. These houses remain unexcavated and are not closely dated so it is unclear whether the present division of the island developed in the later prehistoric period (possibly around 500 BC in the Iron Age) or only when the Norse settlers arrived after AD 800. The impact of prehistoric agriculture on the soils of Papa Stour is at present unknown although recent studies elsewhere in Shetland are beginning to yield interesting results for this period (e.g. Dockrill, this volume).

The agriculture practised by the Norse settlers, as interpreted from archaeological evidence in Papa Stour and elsewhere in the Northern Isles, was not dissimilar to that which was recorded in the earliest surviving documents which discuss agriculture from the eighteenth century. This was a mixed system, based on livestock and crops, with the settlements and arable land separated from common grazings by a town dyke. The arable land was divided into infield and outfield, all within the town dyke. Infield land occupied a limited area around each settlement and was only cultivated by the tenants of the adjacent settlement. It was cultivated every year and was heavily manured. Outfield land comprised extensive areas of rig, long strips of cultivated land, which were not in permanent cultivation and did not receive the quantities of manure used on the infield. Groups or individual rigs worked by the different settlements were mixed together throughout the arable land. This outfield was the run-rig land. The soil was cultivated with the single-stilted plough and crops of six-row barley (bere) and black oats were grown. Barley was the main crop of the well manured infield, oats were grown in the rigs of the outfield. Kail was certainly grown by the seventeenth century but could have been in use much earlier; archaeological evidence for brassica crops is notoriously rare. It appears to have always been grown in enclosed kailyards to protect it from stock during the winter months. We know from Ian Simpson's recent work in Orkney that turf manuring dates back to at least the twelfth century AD in the northern isles and the use of other fertilisers, byre muck and seaweed, can reasonably be assumed.

Eighteenth and Early-Nineteenth Century Developments

From the eighteenth century onwards a variety of agricultural, economic and social developments promoted changes in the agriculture of the island. In agriculture, the potato was introduced and was widely planted by the late eighteenth century. It increasingly replaced the traditional cereal crops because of its higher and more dependable yields. Higher yields were of particular importance at this time because the population of the island was increasing rapidly as landowners increased the number of tenancies to promote fishing. This put pressure on the arable land and led to sub-division of holdings. These major economic and social changes had further, indirect impacts on agriculture. In the smaller sub-divided holdings, the ownership of a plough and plough team became increasingly rare and by the end of the eighteenth century all cultivation was undertaken with the spade only. The promotion of fishing and the expansion of an exchange economy reduced the traditional dependence of the islanders on their own agricultural produce for food. In the nineteenth century, with meal available in the shop, cereal cultivation gradually switched from bere and black oats for human consumption to white oats for livestock fodder.

Later Nineteenth Century 'Improvements'

As a result of the population increase (240 in 1774; 367 in 1841), by the middle of the nineteenth century agriculture in the island had reached a state of crisis. At least this was the view of Sir Arthur Nicholson, one of the two major landowners in the island, when he first promoted an Act of Division in the island in 1846 (see Fenton 1978 for a description of this process). The intention was to divide the common grazings and to re-allocate the arable land into a smaller number of unified holdings. The purpose was to create holdings that could be more readily improved and therefore made more productive. The legal process of division was protracted and continued until 1857.

In view of the considerable effort and expense committed to the division, it is interesting to note that its impact on the geography of the island has been limited. Comparison of the map surveyed by Thomas Irvine of Midbrake (Yell) in 1846 prior to division, with later Ordnance Survey maps of the island reveals that, despite the creation of new fence lines, the basic distribution of arable land remained the same, as did the location of the main settlements. New holdings established by Nicholson soon after the division in the East Biggins, failed to prosper and were abandoned by the early twentieth century. On the ground, traces of the pre-division landscape are even more apparent. The old patchwork of rigs survives in substantial areas of the arable land, largely uncultivated now but preserving the old layout. The underlying cause of the failure of the division to promote agricultural improvement was probably the decline in the population. The Act of Division was promoted at a time when fishing in Shetland was moving away from the old stations with their beaches and peripheral locations which suited the haaf fishery. Sir Arthur Nicholson attempted to develop Papa Stour as a herring station in the mid-nineteenth century but this was short lived as that trade also rapidly polarised to a few major centres. As the fishing declined so did the opportunities to make a living in the island. People again began to rely on local resources for their subsistence but a century of high population had made its mark on the island. The best recorded result is the chronic lack of fuel which was already in short supply in the late eighteenth century. By the later nineteenth century only thin turves were available in the island to burn and peat had to be imported at considerable effort or expense. The factor of the Nicholson estate was unable to obtain sufficient tenants in the island because of the lack of fuel. Emigration was further promoted by changes in agriculture that occurred in the later nineteenth century. Improving landowners, and farmers in Shetland with larger holdings, began to create specialised stock farms to supply the live export market. This development led to the amalgamation of land holdings and a shift from subsistence cereals and potatoes to fodder crops and sown grasses on the arable land. In Papa Stour the shift to stock farming had relatively little impact because of the continuing reduction in the population. Major improved livestock farms were never established in Papa Stour and the overriding impression given by agriculture from the late-nineteenth century onwards is one of progressively declining effort with no major innovations.

The Impact of Changes in Agricultural Practice

From the available evidence, discussed above, it seems likely that the traditional agricultural system that survived into the middle of the twentieth century in Papa Stour had its origins in the Norse settlement of the island after AD 800. This means that, in general terms, the soils of the island have been subject to the same agricultural practices for as much as one thousand years. This conclusion was promising for our research work because it suggested that the soils were highly likely to reflect the types of traditional practices recorded by Fenton. There have, however, been changes over the years in the types of crops grown and the tools used to cultivate the ground. Perhaps of even greater importance is the population peak of the late eighteenth and nineteenth centuries. This must have increased pressure on the local agricultural resources: arable land, grazing land, turf, peat, seaweed and dung. It should be noted that all the early records of agricultural practice, in the *Statistical Accounts* of 1798 and 1845 and in the evidence presented during the process of division after 1846, date from this period of high population. It is the preceding period of relatively low population about which we are largely ignorant.

Given our knowledge of changes in crops, tools and population, the following aspects of agriculture are likely to have changed during the past one thousand years:

- the extent of arable land relative to pasture within the town dyke, reflecting population and demand for crops;
- the extent of arable land in permanent cultivation, reflecting availability of manures and population pressure;
- the rate of application of manures, related to the extent of arable land under cultivation and the availability of manure;
- the availability of different manures, in particular animal dung which reflects the number of beasts owned by a farmer and seaweed which reflects the number of shares into which it is divided.

Analysis of the Cultivation Soils in Papa Stour

Having established, as far as possible, the history of agriculture in Papa Stour, the next stage was to examine the cultivation soils to discover what, if any, of the recorded agricultural practices could be identified from their present day condition. A total of nine soil profiles were sampled for analysis, all within the main town dyke or the separate head dyke of the outset at Hamnavoe. Their characteristics are summarised in Table 2. Samples were collected from these soil profiles and selected chemical and physical properties were analysed. Soil thin sections were prepared from undisturbed blocks of soil and used to study the composition and structure of the soils. Details of the methods used and the results obtained will be published elsewhere. At the time of writing, the analysis of the results has not been completed but sufficient is known to present examples of the findings.

Why Are The Cultivation Soils Deep?

The starting point of our research in Papa Stour was the basic division between the cultivated land with its deep soils and the hill with its shallow, scalped soils. The cultivation soils that we sampled ranged in depth from only 0.25 m in the rig below Olligarth (PS8) to roughly 0.75m in East Biggins, Gardie and the Olligarth Kailyard (PS1, PS2 and PS7). Clearly, soil deepening had not been uniform throughout the arable land. Soil deepening has apparently been caused by the transfer of turves from the hill land. Could our analysis confirm or reject this theory?

Our conclusion is that turf manuring has contributed to the deepening of cultivation soils but at least one other process is involved; this is the natural accumulation of wind-blown sand. Much of the eastern half of Papa Stour is covered in a variable depth of wind-blown sand and its extent corresponds to much of the arable land. Much of the cultivation on the island must therefore originally have taken place in sand. The texture of this sand is very different from that of the turves derived from the western half of the island where local glacial till dominates the soils. Analysis of the texture of the cultivated soils shows that they represent a mixture of the windblown sand and the till-derived turves.

It is possible to calculate how much of each material would have been required to produce the final deepened soil. The results, presented in Table 3, are based on the assumption that some 0.15 m of soil was cultivated prior to the addition of any sand or turf. Two soils, PS1 and PS2, immediately stand out in the table as distinct from the others because of the great depth of sand that has accumulated. This is mixed with lesser quantities of till-derived turves. Both PS1 in the East Biggins and the PS2 at Gardie lie in the path of sand blowing onshore from the Kirk Sand and it is clear that a significant volume of sand has accumulated in the low-lying area between the Kirk Sand and Housa Voe during the period that turf manuring was taking place. Little sand accumulated in any of the other soils examined despite the fact that at least PS4 and PS8 originally developed a wind-blown sand. This sand must reflect an earlier period in the island's history when a much larger area was affected by sand-blow. Turf manuring is indicated in all of the soils except for the uncultivated soil PS9. Six of the profiles accumulated less than 0.25 m of soil from turves but PS5 (North Banks) and PS7 (Olligarth kailyard) stand out with an estimated 0.39 and 0.51 m of turf manure.

Turf manuring was clearly a widespread practice but the turf was not applied evenly over the arable land and only certain areas developed very deep topsoils through this practice.

Is There Any Evidence For Variation In Manuring Practice?

Records from the nineteenth century indicated that the various parts of the arable land were cultivated and manured using different methods. The distinction between the infield and outfield land has already been mentioned and there are also records of the practice of manuring sand soils with seaweed alone. Does any evidence for this variation survive in the soils?

In the previous section, the variable application of turf manure was described with estimated total applications ranging from 0.1 up to 0.51 m. It is not known whether this reflects variation in the rate or frequency of application or perhaps the time period over which manuring took place. Land only recently brought into cultivation during the population peak of the eighteenth/nineteenth centuries might be expected to support shallow soils. At least one of the two deep turf-derived soils can be explained as the result of intensive manuring; this is the kailyard at Olligarth (PS7). Kailyards were traditionally maintained in a highly fertilised state to allow for permanent cropping. The survival of distinct layering in the Olligarth soil is evidence that it accumulated rapidly, especially at the base. The history of the other deep turf-derived soil (PS5) is less clear. It lay within the outset of North Banks and therefore was the exclusive property of that holding and could have been treated as infield, like the kailyard.

A separate line of evidence supports the idea that PS5 and PS7 received more manure than the other soils. All of the cultivation soils contained fragments of burnt peat, derived from hearth ashes and added to the soil as manure, probably mixed with byre muck. The maximum concentrations of peat fragments recorded in soil thin sections reveal that PS5 and PS7 contain much more hearth ash (see Table 4). The results from the four soils at Olligarth (PS6 to PS9) illustrate the variation in peat concentration. The uncultivated soil (PS9) has hardly any fragments and the soil from the plantiecrub (PS6) has almost as few (0.5%). This result from the plantiecrub matches recorded agricultural practice where the only soil improvement undertaken was the addition of fresh turves. The result of 3.3% from the rig soil (PS8) is similar to the other areas of rig sampled (PS1, PS3 and PS4) but is well below the level found in the kailyard.

Conclusions

The striking two-fold division of the soil landscape of Papa Stour has its origins in a natural contrast between local till-derived soils in the west and wind-blown sands in the east. Both of these areas presented limitations for agriculture: the till was shallow and stony, the sand was unstable and prone to drought. At some time, possibly as early as the Iron Age, possibly only after the Norse settlement, turf manuring was introduced. This had two main effects: it addressed the limitations of the wind-blown sand by increasing its stability and ability to retain water, but it also committed farmers to the cultivation of the eastern half of the island by initiating the stripping of the western half. As turf manuring continued, so the contrast between the two halves increased, probably reaching a peak during the period of high population in early nineteenth century.

Within this basic division, our research is beginning to reveal complex variation in the soils of the cultivated land that reflect the details of the traditional agricultural system. We can identify the types and quantities of materials used to fertilise the fields and in some cases suggest the source of these materials. The prospects are good therefore for making the link between the documentary records and the actual soils that resulted from cultivation. There will also be the opportunity to question our interpretation of the documentary record and, in particular, to improve our understanding of the early stages in the development of this soil landscape resulting from agriculture.

References

Crawford, B.E. 1984 'Papa Stour: survival, continuity and change in one Shetland island', in A. Fenton & H. Palsson (eds) *The Northern and Western Isles in the Viking World*. Edinburgh

Dockrill, S.J., Bond, J.M., Milles, A., Simpson, I. & Ambers, J. 1994 'Tofts Ness, Sanday, Orkney. An integrated Study of a Buried Orcadian Landscape', in R. Luff and P. Rowley-Conwy (eds) *Whither Environmental Archaeology*. Oxbow Monograph 38. Oxford

Fenton, A. 1978 *The Northern Isles: Orkney and Shetland*. Edinburgh

Smith, B (ed) 1985 *Shetland Archaeology*. Lerwick

Acknowledgements

We wish to thank the Carnegie Trust for the Universities of Scotland for supporting fieldwork costs (DAD) and the Leverhulme Trust who provided a research grant for the analysis of the soil. George Peterson of Brae kindly shared his memories of agriculture during his childhood in Papa Stour. Finally, we would like to acknowledge Alexander Fenton who suggested that we work in Papa Stour and has provided much useful information and advice.

Table 2. Description Of The Nine Soil Profiles Studied

PS1 East Biggins. A 0.75 m deep cultivation soil within one of a group of pre-division rigs running down slope. Not cultivated within living memory.

PS2 Gardie. A 0.74 m deep cultivation soil exposed through erosion in a low cliff face below Gardie.

PS3 Hamnavoe. A 0.30 m deep cultivation soil in a small area of rigs within the dyke of this early outset. Hamnavoe has been uninhabited since 1909.

PS4 North Banks. A 0.048 m deep cultivation soil within an area of pre-division rigs north of the house. Cultivated until 1960. North Banks was an outset that lay adjacent to the main town dyke.

PS5 North Banks. A 0.60 m deep cultivation soil within an area of pre-enclosure rigs east of the house. Cultivated until 1960.

PS6 Olligarth. A 0.30 m deep cultivation soil within a plantiecrub. The crub was built at the end of the nineteenth century and was probably not used after Olligarth was abandoned in 1940.

PS7 Olligarth. A 0.73 m deep cultivation soil within the Kailyard. The yard was enlarged in the mid-nineteenth century and continued in use for sometime after the house at Olligarth became uninhabited.

PS8 Olligarth. A 0.25 m deep cultivation soil within a group of pre-division rigs. Olligarth was abandoned in 1940.

PS9 Olligarth. An uncultivated peaty soil on the hill above Olligarth, within the town dyke.

Table 3. Estimated Depths Of Sediment Accumulated In Nine Soil Profiles Either From Sand-Blow Or Turf Manuring

Profile	Depth of Topsoil	Original Soil Composition	Depth of Sand Accumulated	Depth of Turf Added
PS1	75	Sand	41	19
PS2	74	Sand	34	25
PS3	30	Till	0	15
PS4	48	Sand	9	24
PS5	60	Till	6	39
PS6	30	Till/Sand	0	15
PS7	73	Till/Sand	7	51
PS8	25	Sand	0	10
PS9	16	Till	0	0

Table 4. Maximum Concentration Of Burnt Peat Fragments In The Nine Soil Profiles

Soil	Maximum Concentration of Burnt Peat (Percent of thin section area)
PS1	3.5
PS2	0.9
PS3	3.9
PS4	3.0
PS5	16.0
PS6	0.5
PS7	10.1
PS8	3.3
PS9	0.2

WHAT FUTURE FOR SHETLAND'S PAST?

Val Turner

The papers in this volume demonstrate the wealth of information which can be uncovered in Shetland by using a variety of approaches. The more successful that this work is, the more Shetland will continue to attract further researchers. In 1995 Shetland Amenity Trust, together with Bradford University, launched the most ambitious research project yet into understanding the factors which shaped Shetland's landscape: the Old Scatness Broch and Jarlshof Environs Project.

Old Scatness Broch and Jarlshof Environs Project

Old Scatness Broch was discovered in 1975 when a cutting was being made in order to build a new road to Sumburgh Airport. The cutting only clipped the edge of the broch, which appeared to be 2-3m high. This edge was examined by the late Tom Henderson, then the curator of the Shetland Museum, together with the Archaeological Society. Their investigations were limited because the society appreciated that the scale of time and resources which would be needed in order to fully excavate a broch were beyond them. As a result the majority of the broch was left largely undisturbed. In 1994 Shetland Amenity Trust took the opportunity to purchase the site, and succeeded in putting together a funding package which allowed the excavation to proceed.

Why should anyone want to excavate a broch site, when Jarlshof is close by, and Mousa, which stands 13m high, is not far away? The main reason is that archaeological methods have changed considerably since the days when Jarlshof and Mousa were excavated (the end of the 19th century – early 20th century) and although some work was carried out on some of the animal bone from Jarlshof, there was no systematic effort to recover either animal or botanical remains, and little appreciation of the type of information which such a study could supply.

There are many questions about brochs to which archaeologists do not have the answers – how they were built, who used them and why (did they belong to a community or a powerful person?), how they related to their surroundings, etc. This research programme will not give archaeologists all the answers – unfortunately archaeology never does – but the relationship of brochs to their surrounding environment is one area which has never been examined in detail before.

The South Mainland of Shetland (the Ness) is an ideal place in which to look at the relationship of brochs to the area around, for several reasons. First there is the wealth of Iron Age remains which are already known in the area. There are three broch site in the immediate vicinity: Old Scatness, Jarlshof and Eastshore. In addition, there are three Iron Age Blockhouse Forts in the same area: Sumburgh Head, Ness of Burgi and Scat Ness. Secondly, the low lying land is covered in a

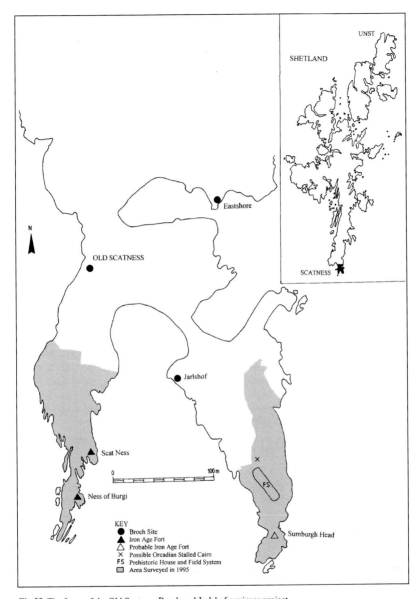

Fig 55. The focus of the Old Scatness Broch and Jarlshof environs project.

considerable depth of windblown sand. This means that the area has always been fertile and good to farm; it also means that the chances of finding charred plant remains, animal bone, pollen, snail and insect remains, together with buried soils, are high. The sand has buried the ruined buildings of succeeding generations of settlers, concealing the stone and thus preventing its reuse. This is very clear at Jarlshof where there are 4000 years of settlement in a very small area. Geophysical survey in the garden of the Sumburgh Hotel (adjacent to Jarlshof), excavations under the airport area during the 1970s, and the discovery of Old Scatness Broch, all suggest that the whole area is full of archaeology just waiting to be discovered, and holding the key to understanding what life in prehistoric times must have been like.

The higher ground of the Scat Ness peninsular and Compass Head supports only a very thin soil. It has not been suitable for intensive farming however, and so the extent of the prehistoric landscape is more easily visible. For all that, it was largely unknown until 1995, when we began our programme of field survey, in order to map the visible prehistoric landscape. This will help our understanding of the brochs because it will help to demonstrate what was happening before and at the time when the brochs were built, and what has been done since to alter the Iron Age landscape.

Some of the most spectacular finds of the survey in 1995 have been the field system (Neolithic or Bronze Age in appearance) which has a house within it, and what may be a Neolithic Bookan-type Cairn, ranged along the hillslope at about 50m above sea level between Sumburgh Head and Compass Head. If the site does prove to be a Bookan-type cairn this will be the first of its kind in Shetland. As a type of site found commonly in Orkney, but so far, never in Shetland, if there are any such cairns here to be found, then it is not surprising that Sumburgh Head would be the likely situation. Early settlers in Shetland must have arrived from Scotland by island hopping (even if they never actually landed), keeping close to islands which they could see all the way from Scotland to Shetland. Higher up the Sumburgh slope still, there is a mass of quarry pits. There are large numbers of prehistoric stone tools found throughout Shetland, but where the stone came from remains, in the majority of cases, a mystery; perhaps these quarries hold the answer. We have also mapped what appear to be the banks of an Iron Age fort which Low reported in his tour of Shetland (Low, 1774) but which largely vanished soon after, when Sumburgh Head Lighthouse was built. All these sites have only been interpreted by observation so far, but geophysics, sampling and limited excavation later in the project will help to confirm or deny our interpretations.

Back on the site at Old Scatness, the 1995 excavation (directed by Steve Dockrill) concentrated on the 19th century croft remains. Crofting in Shetland is well documented and still represents a large part of the oral history tradition. The reason for examining the crofting remains archaeologically in such great detail was to see how what archaeologists can find from the period, particularly in terms of the environmental remains, compares with what we know from historical records. This will allow post-excavation co-ordinator Julie Bond to identify any discrepancies, and then to project these results backwards, to see what assumptions can be made

Fig 56. Aerial view of the site at Old Scatness at the end of the summer, 1997.

141

about the Iron Age environment by comparison. The preliminary results suggest that this method will work well on this particular site, as the levels of preservation seem to be good.

Subsequent excavation in 1996 and 1997 has revealed an unexpected level of survival. There are at least ten buildings ranged around the outside of the broch which stand at least 1.5m high. Some have scarcement ledges visible, which supported an upper storey; one building stands to its original height. The top of its corbelled roof was conclusively identified at the end of the 1997 season, when site supervisor, Alan Braby, literally put his foot in it! It would appear that these buildings represent an Iron Age village which is later than the broch. The next few years promise to be very exciting.

Unst

A foundation year for a second large research project commenced in 1996 in Unst. Here, Shetland Amenity Trust is working together with people and teams from several British Universities and Copenhagen University in order to study Viking Unst. Steffen Stummann Hansen has already carried out preliminary fieldwork and identified about 30 potentially Viking or Norse houses in Unst. Surprisingly few Viking or Norse houses have been excavated in Shetland, or even in Scotland, and we are now taking the opportunity to redress the balance. At the same time, Professor Chris Morris of Glasgow University, will investigate chapel sites dating from a similar period.

Of course it is essential to put this work into the wider context: what type of society did the Vikings find when they arrived? how was it populated? what was the agricultural quality of the land? what influenced their decisions to where to settle? This project will use all the archaeological techniques, as well as historical techniques, such as placename studies, and the examination of udal law, in order to attempt to find some answers to these questions.

Interpretation

Archaeologists are increasingly realising that it is not enough to find answers to research questions, publish them in a journal for archaeologists and then move on to something new. The end product of both these projects is to be a place where the ordinary visitor will want to go. At Old Scatness, we will "rebuild" some of the buildings which have to be removed in order for the excavation to proceed, and we hope to display the Iron Age village, using the information which we get from the excavation, so that the visitor can get an idea of what it might have been like to have lived there. Then, when s/he journeys on to Jarlshof or Mousa, s/he will have far more appreciation of what those sites might have been like. At both Old Scatness and in Unst we hope to build state of the art Interpretive Centres, using virtual reality, or whatever the latest technology is at the turn of the millennium, with lots of ways for the visitor to explore the archaeological material (or replicas of it) for her/himself. Both Centres are planned as places where visitors could pass several happy hours, but then feel inspired to go out throughout Shetland on their own voyages of discovery into the past. Already, Living History demonstrators working at Old Scatness during the excavation season, have kept visitors on the site for several hours as they have made replicas of objects found in the excavation and experimented with ancient technology.

These projects are only the tip of the iceberg of the ideas and plans which the Amenity Trust has for exploring the past. In spite of the recession which the country is in, there are ways and means of funding large scale archaeological projects, through the European Community and the lottery and sources which lie still to be discovered. I am happy to report that I firmly believe that the future for Shetland's past is bright. At the same time Professor Chris Morris of Glasgow University, will investigate chapel sites dating from a similar period

Acknowledgements

I wish to thank all my colleagues in Shetland Amenity Trust for their help and support, also the Department of Archaeological Sciences, University of Bradford, particularly Steve Dockrill and Julie Bond. The major funding bodies for the Old Scatness Project, Phase I, have been: British Academy, European Regional Development Fund (Highlands and Islands Partnership Programme), Shetland Amenity Trust, Shetland Enterprise company, Shetland Islands Council, University of Bradford. The funding bodies for the Unst foundation year were: Historic Scotland, Shetland Amenity Trust, Shetland Enterprise Company and the University of Copenhagen.

References

Low G, 1774, Orkney and Schetland facsimile Inverness, 1985.